Waltz
with Insanity

Mark and Irina,

For your Journey!

Paulette —

Thank you for sharing. It helped me so much!

Waltz with Insanity

A mother's story about the murder of her son and her process of healing through faith.

Paulette Norman

Brown Books
Publishing Group

Waltz with Insanity

© 2004 Paulette Norman

Manufactured in the United States.

For information, please contact:
Brown Books Publishing Group
16200 North Dallas Parkway, Suite 170
Dallas, Texas 75248
www.brownbooks.com
972-381-0009
A New Era in Publishing™

ISBN: 1-933285-49-4
LCCN 2006900643
1 2 3 4 5 6 7 8 9 10

This book is dedicated to God, who has walked with me throughout my life.

And to Wayne, my best friend and husband, who has consistently and persistently shown love and patience.

And last but not least, to Princess Penny, my furry papillon-chihauhua, who was sent to comfort and love me.

I am blessed.

—Paulette

Table of Contents

Foreword

For nearly four decades, I've been listening to people tell their stories. As a pastoral minister for thirteen years and a psychotherapist for twenty-seven more, I've heard tales of joy, inspiration, heartache, and woe. Occasionally someone will ask, "After all this time, you must have heard it all. Are you ever surprised at what you hear?" My answer is, "Never surprised, but often appalled." Paulette Norman's story is in the top five most appalling and ghastly that I've ever heard in my therapy room. To put things in perspective, let me backtrack a bit.

From 1979 to 1987, I was associate director of the Burlingame (California) Counseling Center. Working under the tutelage of Dr. Cecil Osborne, I had many wonderful and challenging experiences with clients from all over the world. In the summer of '87, we moved to Memphis, where I founded the Doyle Family Counseling Center (DFCC) and created a program called Intensive Relational Integration Therapy (IRIT.) The heart of this program consists of thirty hours of one-to-one therapy over the course of one week. We work six nonstop hours, five days straight. In the eighteen years we've been in operation, more than 550 people from over forty states and some foreign countries have taken their turn in IRIT. During the thirty hours of intensive therapy, we visit painful childhood memories, spend some time on cognitive therapy, and include an emphasis on emotive work, including grief and rage work.

As are many of my clients, Paulette was referred to me by another therapist. Mr. Vernon Van Rooy, a fine therapist from Conroe, Texas, knew of my intensive program and thought such a format would be beneficial to Paulette. One year after the gruesome death of her beautiful son McKay, Paulette came to DFCC.

During her IRIT, we covered a lot of ground in Paulette's life: primal pain, childhood hurts, accumulated adult conflicts, and her current crisis—the death of her son—which was, of course, the major focus. Paulette worked hard and made great progress; several months later, she came back for another week and once again worked through more of her hurts, hates, and horrors.

Waltz with Insanity is Paulette's story—a story that could have been entitled *To Hell and Back* because that's what it was and is. Beautifully written, yet horrendous in content, her story is filled with inspiration, hope, and love, and will be a great resource for those who have suffered loss of any kind, and especially for those who have lost children.

As her journey of healing continues, Paulette has honored me with the task of writing this note for her book. My hat is off to you, Paulette, and my heart goes out to you as well.

Don Doyle, DMin, PhD, Memphis, Tennessee
dfcc@earthlink.net
901/757-2347
www.DFCC.net

Chapter One

Before McKay

Push lawn mowers, box fans, wooden clothesline pins, and steeped tea sweetened with Cuban sugar . . . ah, the times of my childhood. We spoke slowly during the long, hot summers. Conserving the small bit of energy that hadn't been drained by the stifling heat was our priority; we never knew who might visit, and we didn't want to be too tired to be courteous and full of Southern charm. *Y'all* and *suppa* and *saaaalad* are the drawled words of my memories. Two of our young friends, Bob and Tim, often brought skillets of fried cracklin' from their family's grocery store. When the cracklin' was freshly fried, Bob and Tim would scoop them up in the top of a cardboard box and run to our house to share. These are the indelible memories of my early years.

Being the oldest of six children, I learned responsibility at an early age. At the age of five, I was allowed to walk by myself to the local grocery and purchase items from my mother's shopping list. I would help the clerk gather the items, and then I'd ride home in the delivery truck. There are four remaining children in my family: Pam, Patsy (Patty Bug), Greg, and Paul. Hugh, the middle child and firstborn son, died in a car accident after graduating from high school.

I was called "Queenie" by my brothers and sisters because I was the oldest and bossiest, and I was expected to look after the other children. I spent a good deal of my early years being the "surrogate mom" to my brothers and sisters. As with many families, we may have appeared ideal from an outsider's point of view, but inside, we lived with a level of dysfunction that to this day we don't discuss. In our quest to appear to be "the perfect family," we children, if not acting perfectly, or in a way that society dictated, would be punished. Today, I can look back on the denial we endured, as many families do, as we thought we enjoyed ourselves, but in reality were unable to share, or to be open and speak freely of losses and unresolved grief. That denial plagued us with rage, anger, and physical ailments.

Magee, the small town where I spent most of my childhood, was a short stop off Highway 49, and could be found about halfway between Jackson and Hattiesburg, Mississippi. References to those larger towns seemed to give a heightened importance to the status of Magee, so we enjoyed telling people where we lived. Another reason the town's name was important to our family was my maiden name: Magee. Although we don't know with any certainty whether a previous descendent was a founding father, the topic still makes for lively debate at family reunions.

We lived in a white, shingled, row house. We had two bedrooms, one bathroom, a living room, a dining room, and a kitchen. The first living room furniture I remember was oversized pieces of red and blue leather-look fabric. In the dining room, we had both an upright and a chest-type freezer—both of which were often stuffed with both frozen food and laundry that had been sprinkled with water and frozen until ironing day. We once updated our home during the course of a single weekend. We caulked windows, painted walls, and added striped curtains and pinch-pleated drapes. After the Duncan Phyfe furniture was purchased, our household took on the look of the middle class. My mother still bemoans her eventual decision to exchange her Duncan Phyfe for Danish Modern. "I must not have been thinking straight with that decision," she has often said.

Chapter One: Before McKay

My dad grew up in a family with eleven children, my mother in a family with five. Consequently, as I was growing up, it seemed we always had a family member in either the hospital or the funeral home. As a small child, I felt as if I were related to almost everyone in town. The first time I heard the phrase "double first cousin," I latched on to it because that's how I could describe my relationship with most of the people in town.

The schooling I received in Magee served me well. I had an array of teachers who positively influenced me, focusing my desires towards becoming a teacher myself. Not all of my school years were smooth sailing, however; I was a small, shy child with a severe school phobia in first grade. My mother did not have a car, and my father worked out of town. There were four of us children at that time. A neighbor, Mr. McBroom, not only delivered his daughter Linda to first grade, he also placed me at my desk more often than not during my first year of school. Mr. McBroom was one of the first gentlemen who showed me that a male could be kind.

The children in my neighborhood called Mr. and Mrs. McBroom "Maw and Paw" McBroom. They were a unique couple: she was a homemaker, he a jeweler. It didn't matter to her how many times the screen door slammed from children running in and out of her two-bedroom, one-bath home that held four of Maw's own children as well. I could identify with their family because it mirrored the living arrangements in my own home at the time. Maw and Paw had a small storage room off the end of their home. It housed the hot water heater . . . and two or three kids if we really stuffed ourselves in tightly. Maw would allow her daughter Linda and two others—if we kept the door open—to sit in the storage room and roast soda crackers over the open flame of a candle.

Animals were a given at Maw and Paw's. The McBrooms welcomed stray dogs and cats at the community feeding bowl that rested outside the back door. One day during my elementary school years, Linda ran into the old horse barn, our pretend schoolhouse that rested halfway between our houses, and said, "My mom has a new pet! Hurry, you have to come quick!" In my mind, I imagined another dog or cat, but much to my surprise upon entering the living room, I saw a chicken perched on the coffee table. They kept the chicken for a while, but it just didn't quite fit in as a house pet. Our homes were in town, not in the country!

Maw and Paw would sit up late at night on the weekends watching TV, cooking homemade divinity, fudge, and popcorn balls, and sewing Barbie clothes. Maw was a lady, Paw was a gentleman, and both of them knew how to have fun. Their dining room walls were lined with plates and spoons displaying the names of the states they had visited. The mementos were a storehouse of information about the states. The kids could recite the capitals, the state birds, and the state flowers of many of the places they had been.

On many weekends, we were allowed the use of the clothesline to build a tent. We would roast hot dogs and marshmallows while the stories flowed. The level of humidity usually determined whether we spent all or only part of the night in our homemade tent.

One special time was during the summer that Maw and Paw agreed to take a carload of kids to Pensacola, Florida. Maw packed fried chicken and potato salad, and we left early one Saturday morning—with ten people stuffed in the car. We had the time of our lives, and I still love reminiscing about that experience today.

I recently spoke with Maw, and when I asked what she had been doing, she told me she had just attended an Elton John and Billy Joel concert. Even though they had four children and lived in a little bitty house, they had a frolicking good time. Their household modeled the way I wanted to bring up my own child someday. That child who would be called McKay.

Another household that I hold in high esteem is Mattie Lou and Hilton Smith's. Their oldest son Smokey and his sister Brenda have been constants in my life. Smokey's words of reassurance have a tenderness that I have leaned on when I have felt lonely. He is nine years my senior and once said, "I held you when you were born." Brenda is a person to whom I can say anything I need to say, and she will not judge me. Their family unit held through the loss of Emmitt, their middle child. I watched their anguish as they fought to go on after the car accident that took his life. I remember one of Mattie Lou's comments: "I went into the bathroom in the funeral home, and I knelt at the toilet and prayed." These are fragments of a time of loss that I still recall. Those precious fragments have ministered to me throughout the years.

The Simmons family helped bring focus to my future. Mary Julia and Shelton's daughter, Dale, has been a friend of mine since fourth grade. This family was never more than an arm's length away, if I could help it. Mary Julia was a driving influence; with the personality of a fireball and her full-of-life attitude, she inspired me to attend college. She had an uncanny way of propelling me forward in my thinking. She was instrumental in teaching me that attitude is everything and anything is possible if I am realistic while still dreaming and doing. The Simmons household was fun! As a teenager, I realized that if I couldn't relate to anyone else, I could relate to Mary Julia.

I remember the heart-wrenching day when Mary Julia suffered from brain stem damage. The doctors never knew what caused the damage, and she was never the same after that. The first time I saw her after the damage, she looked at me with cloudy eyes. A faint recognition of me crossed her face and eyes as she said, "My child, my child, I have no more education." Her words humbled me; she so valued education that even with brain damage she knew one of her greatest prizes was lost.

My childhood years were spent mostly in Mississippi. My roots and memories are deep in the kudzu-covered piney woods. Occasionally, we moved out of state, but only for a summer or a single school year. One of the moves was during my preschool years, when my parents rented a room in the home of an elderly couple in Tennessee. The couple, Rosie and Hughdy, showered me with attention. Rosie had an upright piano, and it felt like a rocket ride when she lifted me to the top of the piano. She would play, and we would sing, "I'm Sittin' on Top of the World." She had two stoves in her kitchen—one wood burning and one modern. I remember standing on a chair at the kitchen table to help Rosie with the stirring and cooking.

Hughdy is the one who took me to the store and purchased my beloved doll named Arbadella. The black doll became my trusted friend, and I would panic if anyone threatened to take her.

When my grandmother Mama Lee lived nearby, I spent as much time as possible with her. She has been my lifelong heroine. She reared five children, three—sometimes four—grandchildren, and helped with two great-grandchildren. She never learned to drive, and she never owned a car. My grandfather was a "lay Baptist minister" who preached in both white and black churches. When my grandfather passed away, my grandmother waited many years to remarry, and only then did she have a home and a car of her own . . . but she still wouldn't drive. Mama Lee shared: she shared her heart and anything else she had. She often said, "I part the dust," meaning that she was willing to give no matter how little she had. I have a vivid memory of her bending over the bathtub, washing the three grandsons' blue jeans by hand because she had no washer or dryer.

Mama Lee lived directly across from the junior high school, and my economics teacher, Mr. Gaither Johnson, once delivered groceries to my grandmother. He told her that "something" had told him that she was in need of food for the boys. She relayed to him that she had spent time on her knees asking for food because she had nothing to feed her grandsons. This, for me, was early evidence that even though Mama Lee was not showered with riches, God made sure she had her basic needs met as she struggled to help others.

Mama Lee always slept in my room with me when she came to visit. She was a loud snorer, so I didn't get much rest. Knowing the nights with her were going to be long ones with little sleep, I would keep her awake as long as I could by talking. Before she dozed off, she would say we needed to pray. I once told her I did not feel right about asking God for material things. She taught me about Solomon and all his glory, and about the lessons he learned; she taught me that the most valuable thing any person could pray for was wisdom.

In later years, Mama Lee lived with my mother in Mississippi. After Mama Lee's second husband passed away, she spent her time on a bus going from one home to the next, visiting her children and grandchildren. I teased her by saying she would probably die on the bus. One day Mama Lee felt she could no longer live in Mississippi. She had a grandson in Georgia who had not been baptized, and she decided to go visit him to find out why. She was a Baptist and to her baptism meant full immersion. She went to visit her grandson, and he was baptized. Before she left for Georgia, she told my mother to give me a message. She said, "Tell Paulette that I will not see her again, but I will be there to meet her when she gets to Heaven." I did not see her again.

I still speak of Mama Lee often. Many years later, when I was teaching Sunday school, I used her as an example. I relayed to my son McKay the beautiful memories of his great-grandmother. The inheritance I received from her in the form of wisdom, kindness, and living a life by example is far more valuable than any money she might have left instead. I am grateful for the sacrificial and unconditional love she showed toward those in need.

The most vivid childhood memory I have of my father's family is the front porch of his parents' home. Mama and Papa Gee rocked for hours in two of the many rocking chairs on the porch. Mama Gee, as we called her, had long, yellowish-gray hair that had "neva" seen a pair of scissors. As we grandchildren would comb her hair, she would remark that the Bible said a woman's hair is her glory. We often gathered on the porch to crank the machines that made homemade ice cream. When Mama Gee made butter, we would churn, and she would rock and teach us things from the Bible. As she rocked, she would say, "Life is but a vapor!"

Mama and Papa Gee had chickens. Mama Gee would stand in the yard with a bucket of corn that we had run through a hand-operated machine. She would yell, "Here chick, here chick, chick, chick, chick," as the hungry chickens came and pecked up the corn. Papa Gee had old wooden crates attached to the side of the outbuildings that were scattered over the farm. The crates were nailed to the wall, and a handful or two of hay was placed inside so the chickens could nest. Each box had a strip of wood running from the ground to the crate. There were cross strips that looked like a little chicken ladder, but I don't recall ever seeing a single chicken using this cute ladder.

Aunt Lavone lived at the top of the hill in our neighborhood in Magee. Her house was really pretty, and the yard was filled with caladiums in the summer. A large, sprawling mimosa tree in her yard hung over the property line between her and Maw and Paw McBroom's yard. As a child, I would climb the tree and read, daydream, doze, and smell the sweetest scents in Heaven when the tree bloomed. Up there in that tree, I would tickle my face with the blooms and lose myself in the clouds.

Not everything in my childhood was a sweet memory. My father was a tyrant whose rage attacks sent me, as a small child, scurrying for my other three siblings. I would frantically herd us to the nearest closet for safety. I remember looking through the small crack that was formed when I carefully opened the door and seeing my mother fighting with my father to keep him from the closet. In later years, we children learned of our father's womanizing.

At my father's hands, I also experienced sexual abuse, suffered from a lack of nurturing, and watched my brothers and sisters be physically abused. I have tried to justify my father's behavioral choices. I have asked others questions and have met with the same responses over and over: his own father was stern and would stay away from home for extended periods of time. Upon his return, his younger children would not know him. But this is not an excuse for the abuse my father heaped upon us; I searched for years for an explanation that would justify his actions, but I haven't found one.

When my mother returned to work after the last two children were born, Nannie Chainy came every day to help with the house. Nannie Chainy and her family farmed cotton a few miles from our home. Their house was raised off the ground and had steps leading to the front porch; under the porch chickens scurried. The front door of Nannie Chainy's house was usually ajar, but we never went inside, although we wondered what was in there. We would just drive up, and she would come out to the car.

Chapter One: Before McKay

She was a great cook. I still recall her flouring chicken by dipping it into egg, then flour, then egg, then flour, and then placing it into the black skillet to fry. The white apron barely made it around her waist, and a tiny bow was tied in the back. The flour would form a light, dusty aura around her as she went about her work. She drank from a fruit jar and ate standing at the counter. When our parents were gone, all of us kids would fix her a place of honor at the table, and that meant a real glass, not a fruit jar, and a meal with us. During these times, even a small sound of an approaching car or person would send her scurrying to the counter with her plate and grabbing for her fruit jar. When Nannie Chainy became too old to care for us and the house, she sent her daughter, Nannie Ola Mae.

While I was in junior high school, an evangelist came to town and set up a tent. The revival services would be held in an area with sawdust covering the ground, and folding chairs were set up for the crowd. The sawdust and the tent fascinated me, and some of us kids decided to go to the revival and see what it was all about. When I attended the revival, I found myself strangely sure, for the first time, of my inability to save myself. The preacher spoke in strong words about the hereafter, and he described it as a Heaven or hell situation. He spoke of decisions and choices that would determine a person's destiny at the point of his or her death. I knew about funeral homes and dying, and I knew that after someone got carried to the funeral home I never saw that person again. In my mind, I considered what my grandmother had taught me about Heaven and hell, and when the altar call was given, I accepted. I wasn't overly emotional; I was simply making the lifelong decisions to trust God and to believe in Heaven, where I wanted to spend my time after dying.

When I was a small child, I remember wearing my pink plastic high heels and accessories to church. The click, click of the heels on the wooden floor still rings in my mind when I remember those times in church. I also attended vacation Bible school once we moved our membership to the Presbyterian church in town and began catechism class. As I went to class, a quiet rebelliousness set in, and I never recited my catechism to the pastor. He made a home visit every Thursday evening to practice catechism and to encourage all of us to be ready to recite it soon. I learned it—I just didn't recite it. I kept quiet about my not reciting the catechism, and only recently did my mother and sisters find out that I didn't receive my Bible, the gift for children who completed the task. I have to giggle when I think about how difficult it must have been for my mother to keep up with six children.

I attended several churches in my life, but the one that sticks out the most in my memory is the local country church of my youth, Sharon Presbyterian. I remember it well—a white wooden structure with beautiful inside woodwork and no air-conditioning, only ceiling fans that turned so slowly as to have a hypnotic effect during the worship service. Each turn of the fan made my sleepy eyes droop further. As I felt myself nodding off, I would try desperately to keep my eyes open because if my dad realized I was getting sleepy, he would thump me on the side of the head.

I did not date until I graduated from high school. One of my first boyfriends was Carl, a boy who grew up about fifteen minutes by car from Magee . . . hours away if you decided to walk and run it for football training, which is exactly what he and his friend Ricky did. Ricky was dating my sister, and Carl came along for the challenge of running from Mendenhall to Magee in one afternoon. I didn't know Ricky or Carl because I had been away at Mississippi College fretting over my Western civilization class and knowing that biology was still looming. When Carl and Ricky arrived at our house the afternoon we met, they were exhausted, and they asked my mother if they could camp out on the front lawn in a tent my two youngest brothers had set up. The next morning while I was leaving for school, Carl looked out of the tent. I thought he was a cute kid—I was nineteen, and he was only fifteen—but he had the most beautiful blue eyes I had ever seen, and he was handsome, sweet, and fun.

Carl and I became fast friends. His parents, Sam and Mamie, earned their living by collecting eggs from approximately 60,000 chickens that lived in chicken houses on their land. Carl jokingly called the chickens "chuckleburs." When I helped Carl pick up the eggs, we would push a buggy that resembled a grocery cart. In our boredom, we would have egg fights, and occasionally Carl would burst into song without any prompting. He sang like Elvis.

At one time, the farm was also home to lots of pigs and horses, and Carl loved the horses. His passion for horses was birthed and nurtured during his childhood. Years later, during one Christmas we shared after many years of marriage, I gave Carl a small plaque that read, "Remember, I loved you when all you possessed was chicken poop between your toes."

The friendship progressed to dating when Carl was fifteen and I was nineteen. We married when he completed high school—he was seventeen, and I was twenty-one. Brother Carl Underhill married us. When we visited his home to make arrangements for the wedding, he and Mrs. Underhill graciously gave us a tour of their home and the little pet cemetery they had at the back of their yard. The cemetery was fenced in, and each pet had a cross or marker to identify its resting place.

Our wedding was sweet. Carl had raised a portion of the money to purchase my rings by picking up glass coke bottles and selling them. I can't explain how tender were the feelings I had when picturing him finding coke bottles to sell in order to buy me a ring. I am humbled by the sincerity of his love. During the wedding, we had Brother Underhill read Romans 8:38–39: "For I am persuaded, that neither death, nor life, nor angels, nor principalities, nor powers, nor things present, nor things to come, nor height, nor depth, nor any other creature, shall be able to separate us from the love of God, which is in Christ Jesus our Lord."

I had attended college for one year, and Carl had a job in the produce department of an A&P food store my Uncle Archie managed. We purchased a small trailer house and a window-unit air conditioner. Each time the compressor of the air conditioner would kick on, the whole trailer would vibrate. I remember once that money was tight, and we had to purchase tires or some high-end item, and we thought we would never pay off the credit card bill. One hot day I was running around the trailer in my underwear and slip, and Carl handed me a stack of bills that had come in the mail. I was so frustrated that I threw them straight up in the air and declared the world an unfair place to live. It was one of the few times Carl got in my face and told me to get a grip.

Life was a struggle, and there was no assistance from our parents. Carl decided he did want a college education, and the best way to secure the money for tuition was by joining the National Guard. When he returned from Fort Polk, Louisiana, he began school at Hinds Junior College.

I completed my degree in education in three-and-a-half years, and soon after, I secured a teaching position. We struggled to pay our way through school, and my parents had bitten off more than they could chew by sending me to Mississippi College. Their intentions were for me to get a good education, but they left out one minor detail: I had to pay for it. My parents simply couldn't provide any of the big frills to six children.

After we married, Carl and I decided not to borrow any money for college. We worked hard to avoid the debt of student loans, and we did, but we didn't have much during those early years. I remember times when we ate nothing more than hot dogs, but we managed to meet the bills, pay tuition, and send the pets, which we had picked up along the way, to the veterinarian. My pets were dear; they gave me something to love and hold.

We still tried to give when we could, like Mama Lee would have wanted. Carl had a big heart and was very generous with what little we had. One evening, Carl brought over George and Missy Hopper to eat with us. We really didn't have enough to share, but they had no money and had been eating only popcorn for days. George is now Dr. Hopper.

Some of my most memorable moments with Carl are the simple, slow, uncomplicated times we spent together—sometimes even in silence. Our fun was simple. Living in rural Mississippi did not afford us many opportunities, so playing with the little piglets or the farm dogs and cats gave me the opportunity to see Carl's soft side. Floating on the river in a johnboat while Carl fished is a memory I return to today when I feel life closing in on me. Dozing off and on in the boat, I'd listen to the gentle lapping of the water. Occasionally, Carl and I would go to a dance, which I really enjoyed. Jackson afforded us a few concerts, some drive-in movies, and the rare treat of climbing the fire tower at night, but most of the fun we had was doing the simple things during a simple time of life. After reflecting on the early years of my life and marriage, I realize that Carl and I were no different from most children, teenagers, or young adults. We had our share of good memories as well as hurtful ones. We had the typical dreams shared by most young couples. We wanted a home, family, money enough to pay the bills, a little left over to save, and a vacation or two.

Carl and I lived in the small town of Clinton. We parked our trailer on a tiny portion of land owned by Margie Gore and her husband, Dr. Sam Gore, who was an art professor at Mississippi College. I had been a doodler for years, but he inspired me to do more. In his small outbuilding between his home and our trailer, I would watch as he sculpted in clay and metal. He traveled with large plastic trash cans in the bed of his truck, and he and his helper would dig clay from the red banks of the Mississippi River. The clay was used in his sculpting classes, and was free for students . . . wonderful for those desperate to save money. Dr. Gore is one of my heroes from Mississippi College.

As expected at a Baptist college, there was mandatory chapel. We had assigned seats, and a proctor took roll. One day I walked into the chapel and realized that the seats were extremely full, and even upper classmen were beginning to line the walls of the auditorium. I thought, "This ought to be good. I wonder who's preaching or singing." Much to my surprise, out onto the stage walked the frailest man I had ever seen. He was elderly, had an elevated shoe on one foot, walked with a cane, and had one ear that was larger than the other. He slowly made his way to the podium, and when he spoke, his voice was as soft as a whisper. He spoke about the dark times—the midnights—of life. He told us about his leg, then about his cauliflower ear. He told this group of know-it-all kids that dark times would one day enter our lives, and he asked us if we had a song we could sing in the midnight of life.

Another time at chapel, a small-framed woman came to speak. She spoke of her husband, who was missing in action in Vietnam. Her request was simple: she asked that we sign a card that could be sent to Hanoi requesting that all prisoners of war or soldiers missing in action be accounted for and then freed. I signed the card. Time passed, and I was told that she had given up hope and had accepted that her husband was killed in action. She moved on with her life and decided to remarry. Before the wedding, word came that her husband was still alive and that he would be coming home, so the town hung a large banner welcoming him.

While Carl completed his course work at Hinds, I taught. We then transferred to Mississippi State University and moved our little home on wheels to Starkville. I was surprised it made the trip. We eventually sold it for the stove, refrigerator, and air conditioner. We did not ask for money for the trailer due to the fact that water had seeped down and under the wood at the front door, and one had to step big in order to keep from putting a foot through the floor. We moved twice to rental properties, and they were quite an experience. In one we had to prop the toilet up with a piece of board in order to level it. The roaches dive-bombed us as we slept. No amount of bug spray affected these large critters.

I taught in a little country school about thirty minutes away from Starkville. The school population lived at poverty level, but the children were sweet and appreciative of the opportunity to learn. The principal was a principal by day and the owner of the Flamingo Club in a neighboring town by night. Carl worked at school through an assistantship and did volunteer work for a veterinarian in his spare time. He needed to make a decision between forestry or veterinary medicine, and he chose forestry; he could not deal with healthy pets being destroyed.

Carl came home one day and commented that he was not leaving Starkville without his master's degree. Within a matter of seconds, I had made a decision as well. "I think I'll get mine too." I wasn't trying to compete with Carl, but I had watched many marriages in which the spouses did not support each other's dreams. Sharing educational goals, I hoped, would help us grow together. The difference in our ages, even though not large, had been a concern of ours prior to marriage. When we had talked about our concerns, I assured Carl that I was committed to the goal of our growing together and not apart. Working towards our master's degrees together was one way I saw to commit to him.

While we were both in school, we were only able to eat out occasionally or sometimes go to a movie. I wanted so badly to see *Gone with the Wind*, so we raided our piggy bank, Horatio, and came up with ticket funds. I still remember the most poignant moment of the movie: when Scarlett stood in the garden vowing never to be hungry again. The tenacity of a Scarlett personality imprinted on my mind.

Before our marriage, and during its early years, I never could determine whether Carl's mom really liked me. Prior to our move to Texas, I told her not to worry about Carl. I assured her I would be there for him, and she seemed to adjust to the move. She even said, "Save a box for me to unpack." She stood on the little slab of concrete they called a front porch, and she waved as we pulled away from their home for the last time before our move to Texas. This is my final memory of her. While Carl was in Texas (he had gone there ahead of me while I finished my school year), his mom had an aneurysm and was placed on life-support systems. The family made the decision to remove the life support, and she passed away.

Eventually, Carl obtained his master's of science in forest biometrics, and I earned mine in education. Deciding it was time for a change, Carl loaded the two dogs in his nonair-conditioned car, I loaded the cat in the little orange Toyota station wagon, and we were off to Texas. I put a leash on the cat and harnessed him down, but he still ran around the car like a wild animal. The vet had given him a sedative so he would sleep, but the pill obviously didn't work. After nightfall, and after a long day of driving, a torrential rainstorm fell, making driving conditions unsafe, so we stopped at a hotel to wait it out. As Carl stood in the pouring rain, we discussed the issue at hand. I was a bit bossy and too long on honesty when I said, "Now, you go in there and tell them we need a room, and we have three pets."

He was drenched by this time, and he said, "Not on your life. We need a room!" So we took a German shepherd, a cat, and another large dog into the hotel—without the management's knowledge. The next morning, I thought we could discreetly remove our pets from the room, so we took them out one by one. I had an old bathmat I wrapped the cat in, and when I turned to look at how well I had covered him, his tail was hanging out! We were young and dumb. Carl commented that removing an elephant would have been just as discreet.

We made it to Willis, Texas, and purchased our first home. It was small, but it was larger than the trailer or the rent houses we had occupied. The first night in our new home, the cat, PC (Privileged Character), went inside a drainage tunnel, and I was frantic that he would not get out. I persuaded Carl to borrow a ladder from a neighbor and go after the cat. He slowly descended the ladder, holding a flashlight. We could hear the cat, so we knew we were on the right track . . . until Carl looked up and saw black widow spiders. He came out of the tunnel much faster than he had gone in and said, "I don't care if you ever see that cat again." My mind said *Back to the drawing board,* so I borrowed a long plank, placed it down into the tunnel, and prayed most of the night that PC had enough brains to walk up it and out. She did.

Carl worked steadily at his job in forestry. After about a year, however, he was less romantic about the job. Frustrated both by snakes in the forest and by incompetent coworkers, he started looking for something else to do. When the Sunday school director from the First Baptist Church of Conroe, the church we had been attending, invited Carl to Houston to see what he did to earn a living, Carl went as soon as he was allowed. This momentous visit moved our lives from forestry to the oil and gas industry. When Carl accepted a job in Houston, we decided to sell our home and move to Conroe so his commute would be shorter.

The oil and gas industry was a different world from forestry. The emphasis was on finding oil and making money ... to find more oil and gas ... to make more money. The lessons we learned in this industry were invaluable, and the ups and downs of the business reminded us that we are not in control; in the blink of an eye, a phone call may arrive, informing us that the job was over. Carl worked for several oil and gas companies, and headhunters called regularly with offers. Carl accepted the offers that were to his advantage.

We found a house to purchase and remodel in Conroe, and it was our home for seven years—the longest period of time I had ever lived in one home. We remodeled in spurts, the final touch being completed just before we sold the house again. We painted, tore out a wall, hung wallpaper, and replaced carpet. We had a brilliant idea about the old packed down and matted gold shag carpet: we'd just rip it up and live on the concrete, which *had* to be cleaner than the carpet. Bad idea: once we pulled out the carpet, the tack strips remained. Carl, the dogs, and I could not remember the tacks when we bounded out of bed each morning! The new carpet's delivery day finally arrived, but when the installers rolled the new carpet out in the long den, it was flawed. The concrete and the tack strips remained for an extra month.

After transferring from New Waverly, I got a job teaching first grade in Conroe. It was during this time that we met and became friends with Hilton and Connie Crawford. My school had an open-concept teaching model, and Connie's classroom was directly across from mine. The Crawfords made their house available for the school faculty's seasonal parties, so we spent time in their house. We also ate out with them occasionally. Connie and Hilton would often invite couples from the school to go to Las Vegas with them. They went a minimum of two to three times a year, and the rooms were always comped. It was not unusual for Connie to ask if Carl and I would like to go. Carl eventually went to Las Vegas and Atlantic City with Hilton, but after one of these trips, Carl came home announcing that he would not be going with Hilton again. I was thrilled because I felt uncomfortable with the trips, even though Carl initially seemed excited to be invited. When he decided to stop going, I didn't express my relief to him because I felt it was his decision to gamble or not—I didn't want to dictate morals.

After Carl's decision, I spoke to Connie in private and told her that he would not be going on a trip with Hilton again. I told Connie that the choice not to attend the trips was not a reflection of how we felt about them—I assured her that we cared for them, but we would not participate in the gambling. She simply commented that she would tell Hilton. Carl eventually told me that his decision not to attend another gambling expedition was that he was extremely uncomfortable with Hilton's friends, one in particular who really disturbed Carl.

Time passed and I thought life was good, but one day while I was painting, Carl entered the room and said, "I feel unfulfilled in this marriage." My head whirled. *What?* I couldn't identify with these feelings, as I felt very complete: I had marriage, spiritual life, church work, pets, painting, exercise, piano, reading, walking, teaching, and volunteer work. I asked Carl what would make him feel fulfilled, and he said, "Having a child." I agreed with him.

Soon after, Carl and I took a trip to Cancun, but we broke most of the rules about where or where not to eat. Consequently, we were quite green when we arrived back in the US. I made a quick trip to the doctor, and then Carl was on the road again. He always prided himself on not going to the doctor or hospital. After several weeks of misery, however, I told Carl he had to take me to Mexico to see a doctor who would be familiar with my symptoms, since the doctor in the US didn't know what was wrong. Carl took me to my OB/GYN instead. Dr. Meyer performed several tests, and then decided to do a pregnancy test. I was three months pregnant! This was a great shock since nausea had been the only symptom I experienced. I changed my diet and ate mostly raw fruits and vegetables, but I did have one food vice: chocolate milkshakes. Carl seemed to enjoy them as much as I did, and we both steadily gained weight—about thirty pounds each.

Chapter One: Before McKay

We were a mixture of excitement and confusion. Carl seemed to settle in and feel fulfilled. I became moody, cried a lot, and paced the floor at night. I was a body full of anxiety as my mind raced and worried about how to keep a child safe in this crazy world. One summer day when I was running around the house barefoot, Carl called from a northern state where he was working, and he told me he had been laid off. I didn't understand why his company would call him while he was out of town to deliver the news of his layoff. Actually, the company hadn't called, but an employee had gone into the boardroom during lunch hour, and he read termination packages of employees who were being laid off. That employee called Carl and told him. We needed to keep our health insurance for the pregnancy, so Carl had to use a ploy to keep his job.

By this time, we had learned that the oil and gas industry could be very volatile, and I had encouraged Carl to remain indispensable to his company, and that meant he had to carry something of importance with him at all times as a hedge for extending the longevity of his job. If he were in the process of working on something of importance, it would be tougher for the company to let him go. Carl called the office, and they relayed to him that he was laid off with a severance package. He told them there was a dumpster outside his room, and he would toss his briefcase into it before he came home. Then he told them what was in the case, and they agreed to talk. They hired Carl as contract labor, which allowed him to come home and to open an oil and gas business of our own.

The pregnancy took its toll on me, and it also took its toll on our marriage. I was so distraught about how I would protect our baby that safety and security—my issues—plagued me day and night. I did not talk to anyone about my concerns, and even Carl only knew only a small portion of my thoughts and prayers. One day I became so distraught, I lay on the floor crying and asking God to not make me go through this, but it was His will, not mine. I surrendered.

Carl, at times, would become so frustrated with me that he would tell me he was going to take the baby and leave. I did not cry very often in front of Carl because I was embarrassed, and at that time in my life, I felt crying was a sign of weakness. When we were small, my siblings and I were afraid to cry due to my father's threats of what would happen if we did, and this lesson had stayed with me. The amount of crying I was doing was so unusual that Carl told Dr. Meyer that I was not the wife he knew and that he had never seen me in such a state of emotion. Carl, on the other hand, was calm and confident about the baby. He often reassured me: "If you will love this baby as much as you do these puppy dogs and kitty cats, then it will be great!"

There were times when I felt a closeness to Carl I had not felt before my pregnancy. He continued to be supportive, and showed his dedication to me by sitting up with me at night when I could not sleep, and in the latter part of my pregnancy, when I slept on the sofa, he slept on the floor beside me. I read the Bible and prayed, and I repeated scriptures in my head to help these attacks of anxiety about the baby. Since then, I have realized that the scriptures were a "fix" to help me through the tough times, and I am glad I had them to support me during those times of extreme, intense anxiety.

Choosing a name for a baby is not as easy as it seems, we found. We wanted to find a name both of us loved, and we wanted the full name to have a nice ring to it when spoken. I fretted over a boy's name, but I had no trouble choosing for a girl. Carl and I both agreed that Mary Lee, my grandmother's name, would be wonderful. The boy's name was not as easy. I liked Samuel, which is Carl's first name, but I could not find a name to put with it. I called my mother one evening and asked her if she could prepare a list of family names she could remember. She said a few out loud, and when I heard *McKay*, I said, "That's it!" Carl was outside visiting with a neighbor, and I joined them and asked Carl how he felt about Samuel McKay. He liked it, and so did I.

Since I was a thirty-three-year-old, pregnant for the first time, many of our friends threw baby showers. Our friends were elated and didn't know of the struggles Carl and I were experiencing in our marriage. I appreciated their support and gifts.

Chapter One: Before McKay

While I was pregnant, Carl gave me a diamond that I recently had reset so I can wear it more often. It is truly one of my most valued gifts from him, and it reminds me of our friendship and love during those years. When I look at the diamond now, I still see the twinkle in Carl's eyes when he thought about McKay. Another memory snapshot is when Carl came up behind me in a store and wrapped his arms around my big stomach, hugging me and the baby.

Dr. Meyer once asked me if I believed in providence. I told him I did, and he said, "This baby is providence." He reassured me that when one is given more to love, the capacity to love grows. I held on to those words.

As the day of delivery grew near, I began to experience spots in front of my eyes. I went to lunch with a friend who was also pregnant, and I told her I needed to get my eyes checked after the baby was born. I had difficulty driving myself home that day. The next morning, during a scheduled doctor's appointment, Dr. Meyer found that I had developed toxemia. He sent me home to bed for the next twenty-four hours, and asked me to return the next day for another checkup. The doctor had told Carl to pack his bag in advance and to store it in the car, just in case. Of course, Carl didn't pack the bag, and when the time came, he had to rush home for it.

I remember some of the funny things that happened in the labor room. I wasn't in any pain, even though I was hooked up to a drip to induce labor. I kept thinking, There's nothing to this. I had prayed in earnest while Carl had gone home for his bag—I was afraid, and I felt very alone. I was reminded of Christ and when he was in the garden alone. After hours of no pain, I was beginning to think that God had really heard my prayers, and that I was being spared any pain in childbirth. I was naïve. Dr. Meyer entered the room, seemed frustrated, walked straight to the machine that monitored the drip, and turned up the dial. That's when I knew I was in for a long day.

Hours of the drip produced very little response, and I was no closer to delivering the baby. When I could bear the pain no longer, I grabbed Carl by the shirt collar and told him to get me some relief. Dr. Meyer gave me what he called a two-martini lunch: Demerol. It was wonderful.

Later that night, Carl went to Dr. Meyer and said he was ready to get this over with. The baby's heart rate was dropping, and the doctor agreed that it was time. The assisting physician's son Michael was in my first-grade classroom, and while I was under the influence of childbirth, I proceeded to berate Dr. Meyer for not spending enough time with Michael. I also told him he should give up smoking. I remember telling myself to breathe, or I would die. Carl was with me throughout the delivery. I remember watching his intensely blue eyes as he watched our son being brought into the world.

I clung to Carl after the delivery; I didn't want to be separated from him. In the recovery room, Dr. Meyer stayed with me. He was concerned that I would not bond with McKay, and he reminded me of an old animal doctor as he rubbed McKay up and down my body. I wanted to laugh, cry, and give thanks for a wonderful doctor who cared enough to nurture me through pregnancy, childbirth, and bonding with McKay. I had never experienced such caring from a physician. Over and over, when I had expressed concern that Carl and I would lose our closeness after the baby was born, Dr. Meyer had reassured me that we would be fine.

We are here for a period of time . . .
but not forever.
—*Wayne*

Chapter Two
My Greatest Prize

How can a mother give an accurate account of her child if she doesn't know how he felt when he spied his first grasshopper or how proud or afraid he felt on his first plane ride alone to his aunt's house in Mississippi? Or what possessed him at age four to pull a chair into the kitchen, fill a cup with water, pour garlic powder in the cup of water, place it in the microwave, and turn on the microwave, causing a garlic smell to be propelled throughout the house? Or his rationale for collecting bird feathers and rocks and placing them in leftover Styrofoam burger containers? Or what was in his heart and mind as he would hold my cheeks with the palms of his hands until my mouth would pucker, and then kiss me squarely on the lips and say "mawing" or "I luz you" in his little Mississippi drawl?

I stand in awe among the memories and the impact this little person had on my life. A family friend once remarked as Carl and I were relaying stories about McKay that the memories we were making with McKay were an ointment for the soul. As I remember moments that have been pushed far, far back, I remind myself that my soul is being anointed.

McKay was born sucking his thumb. The doctors said it was the sign of a good baby, and they were right. McKay's eyes were large pools of blue that drew me into his world. The batting of his extra-long eyelashes reminded me of the slow, relaxing, summer playtimes under the weeping willow trees in Mississippi. His eyelashes were like the long, swooping branches of the tree that stood in the backyard of my Uncle Daniel and Aunt Barbara's home. I was reminded of the branches' soft, swishing sound as they swept across the ground when the wind blew.

I would walk in the misting rain with McKay when he was just an infant. I wanted him to feel the mist on his face and know he was alive and that life could be gentle and loving. When my brother died in a car accident, I was unable to enjoy walking in the rain for over a year. I did not notice the soothing sound of drops falling steadily on my umbrella, could not feel the cool of the mist in my face; I missed it. I wanted McKay to experience what I had missed. As we walked, I talked to him as if he were an adult. I would tell him of life, and I'd talk about how much fun we would have when he was able to walk and talk and tell me about himself.

Reading was an important part of my life. I read to my children at school, and I knew the value of reading to a young child. I wanted McKay to have a successful and positive experience in school, and I felt that reading aloud to him was essential. When he was a toddler, I read aloud to him as he played with his toys. Every so often, he would run over to the book and look at the pictures, then he would hurry off to play again. At first, I was frustrated because I wanted to hold him as I read to him, but his playing while I read was the only arrangement that would work with McKay. I adjusted. I didn't forfeit the time just because it was not the traditional "sitting in the rocking chair with baby on lap while reading a story." The books that were among his favorites were *Charlotte's Web, The Velveteen Rabbit, The Steadfast Tin Soldier,* and *I'll Love You Forever.* His favorite book to read with his dad was *Just Me and My Dad.*

I like rocking chairs, and we had them in many rooms in our home. I think a baby should be rocked. Rocking is a form of nurturing, and even at the age of twelve, McKay still enjoyed being rocked. Once we hauled a rocker to Sunday school. The class I taught usually had forty to sixty in attendance on any given Sunday morning, and I enjoyed being creative when I taught. We began one class with McKay in my lap while I rocked him and read *I'll Love You Forever.* In the mornings, he would race me to the kitchen. If he beat me to the kitchen, I would hear the rocker creaking as he went back and forth, back and forth. Most mornings he wanted to be rocked; it was our time together.

From the beginning, McKay was an easy child. He didn't spit up much, and before he even learned to walk, he could blow his nose with a tissue. Once, when he developed a rash, the doctor said we were bathing him too much. The doctor, who called McKay "old blue eyes," said a little dirt would not hurt, so we stopped giving him so many baths.

Carl and McKay enjoyed a mutual love for shopping. On one trip when McKay was about four, they purchased a bow and arrow set from the dime store. I told Carl I didn't think he should have purchased that type of toy for McKay, but Carl said it would be fine. McKay unwrapped the bow and arrows and seemed quietly occupied, so I went about doing some household chores. I heard Carl yelp and hang up the phone he was using in his office. When we met, he was holding one hand over an eye. I asked him what had happened, and he said while he was talking to a client, McKay twirled round and round, and then shot an arrow from the bow. McKay was not aiming for him, but the arrow hit Carl right in the eye. I had to remind Carl that McKay's first word was "Dada."

My mother felt that McKay needed a blanket just his size, so every now and then, she would call to ask how much he had grown, and if there was a substantial increase in height, she would make another quilt for him. Her designs ranged from all sorts of different subjects to many varied color schemes. McKay grew to look forward to the quilts she made. We tracked his growth by marking his height with a pencil on the inside of his closet door, and when he had grown significantly, we knew a new quilt was in the works.

The school years from day care to seventh grade were full of memorable moments. McKay was blessed with very loving and highly skilled teachers.

When he was small, Carl and I would ask him where he was going as he stood ready to go to school. Dressed up, hair combed and parted, clothes matching, he would say, "I have to go to school and play with those children."

Most mornings before school, I would cook breakfast. If McKay was groggy, I would cook grits, and we would have a grit-spitting fight before breakfast was complete. After that, he would be wide-awake, full of life, and ready to go to school for fun and games. McKay brought out the child in me. We were not only parent and child, but because he was an only child, I was his playmate, too. I enjoyed having fun with McKay.

During kindergarten at Glenwood, his big challenge was to be courageous enough to ride the playground trolley. His confidence level soared the day he climbed up high, held on for a ride down the cable, touched the ground with precision, jumped up, and did it again. He spent his life meeting and overcoming challenges this way.

One afternoon after kindergarten, I received a phone call from the 9-1-1 dispatcher, who informed me that she had received a 9-1-1 call from our home phone. I politely told her no one had called 9-1-1. She asked me if I had a child at home to which I replied, "Yes, but he wouldn't—"; before I could complete my sentence, my eyes met McKay's eyes, and I ended the conversation with, "Oh, yes, he would, and I am so sorry." It just so happened that a little friend of McKay's at kindergarten would make a detour during his bathroom trips. From the phone nearest the school kitchen, he would dial 9-1-1 and then run. After several visits from the police department, the school finally caught the culprit and put a stop to his pranks. McKay learned more at kindergarten than just ABCs.

We once took McKay on a camping trip, and we had unrealistic dreams of becoming one with the great outdoors. Carl purchased a tent and supplies, and we loaded everything and were off to give camping a try. We built a campfire, and McKay began to experiment with the different foods and how they tasted over the campfire. His greatest find for the trip was roasted "smarshmallows," as he called them, with a touch of mustard. We were having a really good time until it was time to go to bed and we began to hear the coyotes. McKay became frightened, and Carl and I, while not admitting it to McKay, were nervous as well. After a respectable length of time, we loaded everything up and went home.

After McKay's birth, I did not return to teaching but began working with Carl in the oil and gas industry. I had mixed emotions about putting my career and its benefits on hold, but I didn't feel it would be fair to either McKay or my students if I tried to teach and mother. We hired a lady named Miss Doris to care for McKay. I was grateful that I had the opportunity to work with Carl, and I had the flexibility to come and go when I needed. I spent more time with McKay this way than I would have if I had continued with my teaching career.

In first grade, his teacher, Mrs. Loftin, called and told me McKay had a very large glass jug of pennies at school. I was shocked; I knew the jug she referred to—his grandmother had given it to him—but I hadn't seen McKay leave the house with it! I asked his teacher how he got them to school, and she replied that it was simple: his backpack.

McKay's backpack held a great resource of items, including one time a bullwhip for show-and-tell. When his turn came to share, he asked if he could demonstrate how a whip could pop. His teacher, Mrs. Loftin, taught with me before McKay was born. I had given her fair warning that McKay was ingenious and liked show-and-tell, and I asked her to please, please correct him when needed. Nevertheless, the whip came out of the backpack and the demonstration ensued. The tail of the whip caught a blue streamer that was hanging from a paper rainbow, and the streamer went flying. McKay's only comment? "I never did like blue!"

One afternoon, he returned from school crying. As I tried to understand why he was so upset, all I could make out was that the teacher said he was, "Scrubbling." I asked him several times what he was saying, and every time he repeated, "She said I was scrubbling!" This went on for a while . . . until I thought to ask what he was doing when the teacher told him this. Only when he said he had been writing did I realize the teacher had said he was "scribbling."

When he was in first grade, McKay received his first pair of penny loafers—the type of shoes that actually held a shiny penny. They were his Sunday shoes and shopping shoes. He liked to wear them shopping because be would find a hard surface and tap dance. Carl and I would help him locate a floor that had a mirror nearby so he could watch himself as he danced. He was a fan of Sammy Davis, Jr., and he would mimic his dance steps as well as those of the children who danced on the streets in New Orleans. Today, I hold McKay's shoes and tell myself that I have not imagined him being here with me.

In second grade, McKay began to develop his reading skills, but he struggled and struggled with spelling and reading. It took extra work on his part to keep up in school. He studied in the afternoon and evening after school. If he felt his grades were not where he wanted them to be, he would ask for extra work in order to make a better grade. This was his way of keeping his mom and dad happy. His teacher, Miss Thomas, was diligent and focused on the class and their needs, and she was a great help to McKay.

McKay enjoyed projects; once he completed a school project on Montana and fashioned it after the movie *City Slickers*. He even dressed the part to present his project. He wore a hat, jeans, boots, and a bandana around his neck. He was mature about deciding what materials he needed for his project, and he completed all the work himself. I was tempted to step in and help, but then it wouldn't have been his creation.

In third grade, McKay was required to build a motorized invention. He built a robot dog that looked like his favorite pet, Fleetwood (a Brittany spaniel). He used a cardboard box for the body and a smaller box for the head. When he showed his invention, his teacher Carmelita Hayes later told me, the class was sitting in a circle. No one expected the cardboard box dog to move, not even Mrs. Hayes, herself. The children scampered and yelled as the dog moved toward them. McKay had placed a remote-control car under the box, and the robot dog moved via the car's controls.

One year, the intermediate school celebrated Grandparent's Day. McKay knew it was a long drive for family (none of our immediate family lied within driving distance of the school), so he invited his elementary school principal, Mrs. Wilkinson. He packed a lunch for himself and Mrs. Wilkinson. He took large quantities of food, and I didn't help him pack at all—this was his moment. He used a large brown grocery bag to haul in the feast, and Mrs. Wilkinson enjoyed herself so much, we still refer to her as McKay's fill-in grandmother.

McKay went to Geisinger Elementary and then to Reaves Intermediate. He was an average student who spent time on his schoolwork, and he was a little boy who loved to do little boy things. He once came home asking for me to go to school and fix a situation for him. He said: "Just get up in the morning and come to school with me and talk with that teacher."

I told him, "No, you get all dressed up in the morning, and go in and plead your case yourself. You got yourself into this, not me. I will not bail you out when you have displayed inappropriate behavior or made bad choices. If you did something you shouldn't have, then apologize, but understand that saying you're sorry will not always take away the consequences." This seemed harsh to him, and it may seem harsh to some parents reading this, but I knew he needed to learn accountability for his behavior. This did not mean that I would shirk my responsibility as his advocate when appropriate.

I have never been a great—or even consistently good—cook, but I cooked for McKay. If the piano or my artwork called to me, I would leave the stove and forget about the cooking. McKay would call out "Woman, what are you burning?" If dinner was not to his liking, he would ask, "KFC?" We shared some favorite foods that Carl did not enjoy—tuna fish and peanut butter. As Carl would drive off to work, McKay would yell, "Tuna or peanut butter!" and we would share a sandwich while talking or watching *Gone with the Wind* or Andy and Barney of Mayberry.

McKay began to play the piano as soon as he could sit in my lap. He played independently as soon as he could maneuver the climb to the top of the bench. At an early age, he was able to play a few things for himself, and he sat at the piano for extended periods of time, far beyond the normal attention span for his age. I taught him for two years. Once, when he was in first grade, we planned a weekend trip. As we were walking out the door, he said he needed to play a song for us. He ran back to the piano and played like I had not heard before. Carl was puzzled and so was I. Carl asked me if I had taught McKay the song, and I said I had not. At that moment, I gained new insight into the musical ability of this person I called son.

On my side of the family, we have what we call honky-tonk musicians. McKay would say, "I am playing honking tonking," and on rare occasions, when his mood was right, he would place his feet on the keys and be Jerry Lee Lewis. I would laugh to myself and think, *The nut doesn't fall too far from the tree!*

I painted so often at my kitchen table that friends have remarked they wouldn't know what to do if the table weren't covered with paint and glitter. Our master bedroom had a view of the area where I painted, and at night when McKay couldn't sleep, he would quietly descend the back stairwell. I would watch him from my bedroom windows as he stood at my easel and painted with great intensity. I was at ease with him at my easel because oil painting is forgiving; anything he chose to paint could be corrected. I would watch as he lost himself in the painting. I felt honored to watch him from the sidelines.

McKay's Christmas lists were usually unique. He requested a harmonica when he was four, a violin at age five, drums at six, a regular guitar at age seven, a red electric guitar at ten, and the keyboard at eleven. In fifth grade, he decided he wanted to play the saxophone. Carl wanted to purchase the sax, but I felt it needed to be rented until we knew if McKay were truly interested. The sax was an instrument played with more than just the hands, and McKay's greatest successes were with instruments he played with his hands. The sax was rented, and each afternoon McKay walked up and down the neighborhood streets playing it. He visited a few homes for a guest appearance. After a few weeks, the saxophone was returned to the music store. Thank goodness it was only rented.

The harmonica was a handy instrument. It fit nicely in his pocket and was ready in a snap if he decided to play. One time, he played a tune for his dad as they were riding to town. Carl came inside, shaking his head, but smiling. He remarked that McKay played an unrecognizable tune on his harmonica, then wiped his eye and said, "That one even makes me cry!"

The violin was the instrument that he longed for. His face on Christmas morning was one of sheer delight and shock when he realized his longing was met. He screeched and scratched on the violin for years. I also remember the look on his face when he realized he was not a "natural" on the violin. It frustrated him that the violin was such a challenge. Even with lessons, it was still a challenge.

He received a keyboard for Christmas when he was eleven. He used it both for playing and for creating sound effects. The most real sound that would vibrate the walls was that of a motorcycle. The different instrument sounds held his interest for long periods of time, and I was happy when he could find something that interested him for more than a few minutes. Even though he kept the noise level high, I thought it was positive that he could settle down to one activity for a period of time.

He kept his drums in his hidey hole or in his playroom, but even their being far from our living area didn't do much to lessen the noise level when he played. McKay had several friends who would visit and play different instruments, trying to sound like a band. The back stairwell was near the playroom, and it wasn't unusual for children from the neighborhood to be upstairs playing instruments, while others would slide down the back stairwell in a cardboard box . . . all while I was at the foot of the stairwell, painting.

When he was about twelve, McKay wanted to stop piano lessons. He asked, "If I learn the violin, can I quit piano lessons?" I was a bit surprised, as he seemed very diligent about practicing and going to lessons. In fact, when he took piano lessons from Mrs. Lum, I once delivered him to his lesson on the wrong day. He went inside to the studio filled with busts of old composers and gave himself a lesson! However, I felt that letting him quit was a fair trade since he had played the piano for six years. I also realized he hadn't mastered a single song on the violin thus far, so piano lessons were not in jeopardy. He was suffering burnout and looking for a reason to quit even though he was a good pianist. He found his reason: his teacher had hurt her arm, so she replaced her pointer with a thin tomato stake. McKay told me the stake got on his nerves, and he wanted to play the violin anyway. He found his old practice book and set about teaching himself the violin. Within a few days, he learned "Amazing Grace." I'm glad we stopped piano and let him learn the violin. He was a gifted and determined player.

As with most children, McKay enjoyed campfires and fire in general. In fourth grade, he asked for a Bunsen burner for his birthday. Of course we refused, but that didn't end his love of fire. On that year, before his birthday, an ice storm moved in. We lost electricity, but we used our natural gas fireplace to obtain heat. McKay was at an age where he assumed some household responsibilities, and he asked to light the fireplace in the den. When he bent over to turn the gas valve, he raised the hand that was holding the lit starter. He accidentally burned a small area on the mantle of the fireplace. I knew something had happened, because in the past, McKay would rush to the piano and play rapidly if he was upset. He played frantically that day.

Carl telephoned shortly after the incident, asking when I was coming to work. McKay was to spend the day with friends. I told him what had happened with the fireplace mantle, and Carl said he needed to tell me something else, but didn't exactly know how to do it. He explained that when he was above the garage in the attic, he had noticed that the room looked different. He saw that McKay had created his own laboratory with a homemade Bunsen burner. The burner was fashioned from a piece of clothes hanger, and burned matches were lying underneath. I was shocked. I didn't want to sound alarmed to Carl, so I spoke in the softest voice I could muster, but inside, I wanted to scream, *He could have been burned!* I remembered the suffering my sister experienced when she was burned.

Carl decided the best way to deal with a firebug was to give him fire. Carl and McKay went to the grocery store and came back with a big old-fashioned box of strike-anywhere matches. McKay was allowed to strike every match in the box. Carl supervised him as he struck matches on the box, the concrete, and the zipper of his jeans. I decided that this was a guy thing, so I went inside. After that, we did not have any more frightening fire incidents with McKay.

Neither Carl nor I had grown up taking yearly family vacations. After discussing the importance of giving McKay the opportunity to see more at an early age than we had seen, we began to plan vacations. We took trips to Arkansas to fish, we went to Disneyland, and we went to New Orleans. My mother and McKay's Aunt Patty Bug took him to Memphis to visit Graceland. We went to New York for Christmas, Carl and McKay went with a school group to Washington DC, and McKay and his dad went to Space Camp. My memory holds many snapshots of these times.

We took McKay to New York City, where he saw Santa in Times Square, saw the Statue of Liberty ("Liverty"), rode the subway, saw the *Messiah* at Carnegie Hall, and went to the Broadway musical, *The Secret Garden*. *The Secret Garden* was a gift from the family who was traveling with us. Little did they know that McKay had been introduced to the story once when he was watching PBS television. This family had no idea of how special this story would become and how it would play out in McKay's life. We took the tour of the big toy store in New York, and I was amazed at the number of children that could be packed into one building of toys. After the speedy taxi rides in New York, McKay came home saying that he did not want to be a doctor after all—he had decided to become a taxi driver instead. He left New York determined to return.

Each child has ways of expressing himself that are unique to his world and his needs. McKay was no different: he would say *pinecorns* for pinecones and *mama dos* for snickerdoodle cookies. Many times he would refer to me as "Woman" instead of "Mom." He had a fetish for little white sugar donuts. He collected sunshades; we would borrow each other's. When he would tire of me and the activities of the moment, he would say "I need a drake [break]." McKay enjoyed clothes and shoes and he liked to be sure everything he wore matched.

One of McKay's ways to escape into himself was spending time in the tree swing or in the barn, a place he always loved to play. There was a hodgepodge of tools, leftover building materials, and various odds and ends. When McKay brainstormed new ideas, he usually started with a sketch.

The sketches were sometimes intricately detailed, depending on how much time he had to spend. He would call them his "projects." Carl's barn had a little of everything because he was not the type to clean out and throw away. Many of the tools he had purchased were in their original wrappings. Everyone in the neighborhood was welcome to use the tools; in fact, they referred to Carl's barn as Everett's Hardware.

One particular project, a pair of oversized wings McKay made, were a source of endless frustration to him. He could not understand why they would not allow him to fly. He made them from lightweight material that was stacked in the middle of the floor. After I helped him attach the wings to his arms, he waved his arms and watched his feet. I could not help but giggle because he was honesty waiting for his feet to leave the floor. They didn't.

McKay tried to build a motor scooter by taking apart an old bicycle. He worked and worked to build the scooter, and when it was finished, he spray painted the body with many cans of paint. It didn't win any road races, but it was an achievement of which he was proud.

As a mere four-year-old, he went to the garage and found a battery-operated drill and proceeded to remove the taillight covers from my car. He asked Carl if he would like for him to remove the covers from his truck; Carl was shocked at McKay's ability to hold the drill and his ability to use it proficiently. Once, Carl purchased McKay a battery-operated jeep, a small-sized type in which the child is able to maneuver and drive the vehicle. McKay drove it for a short period of time, then went to the garage and put the drill to use—he disassembled the jeep.

McKay's goal for the Christmas of 1995 was to build everyone's gift. He planned to use the leftover slats of fencing stored in the barn. He drew sketches and measured and sawed and hammered. He designed a magazine rack and bookstand and then built it and liked what he saw, so he gave it to one of his aunts.

Every once in a while, we would go shopping in the kitchen aisles of a store, and we'd come out with something different to use when we cooked. Our goodies ranged from a Mickey and Minnie waffle iron to a wok. The wok was a whole new adventure for Carl and McKay. It rated an immediate trip to the grocery store to purchase vegetables, chicken, bean sprouts, and soy sauce. We called our meals "woking" time, and for a period of time, Carl and McKay cooked several times a week. The fun was in watching Carl and McKay shop, chop, and wok. For Christmas, I made Carl a memory book of photos for the year. Included in the book was a picture of cooking with the wok. McKay would play butler and server when he helped with dinner, and he would take orders and serve. Of course, he expected a tip!

Each summer, McKay went to visit Aunt Pam and Uncle Terry who live about twenty miles inland from Gulfport and Biloxi. He played with the farm animals and talked his aunt into establishing a petting zoo so when she retired there would be something to do in order to keep her busy. The farm animals varied from trip to trip. She had one cow named Forrest—Forrest Gump—that would not be sold. The aunt kept geese on the pond, and she provided them with nesting areas. There were horses and mules, cats and dogs, and an array of other animals, each with its own domain. The aunt once picked up a stray dog from the side of the road, and she named him PLP—Poor Little Pup—PL for short. He was not the friendliest dog any of us had ever met, to say the least, and McKay and I kept a respectful distance from him.

The family's cat, Bubbles (Bubs for short), was an odd sort of cat who knew he held ownership of the farmhouse. Bubs had his regular trips to the vet, and when the vet announced that Bubs would not live due to an incurable virus, the aunt rubbed him down with Vicks Vapor Rub and wrapped him in a towel for days. He lived for years after this treatment, and to this day, the aunt swears by Vicks.

When McKay was a toddler, he chased Bubbles under a chair. When he went for Bubs, Bubs bit him. McKay's response was based on instinct: he bit Bubs back. Carl and I had already spent a lot of time trying to break McKay of biting. He would bite when he wanted to show affection, anger, or just any old feeling that came along. I was beside myself one day when the nursery school teacher told me McKay had bitten another child. I apologized profusely, but when I gave McKay his evening bath, I noticed a big bite mark on his back.

McKay enjoyed the peacocks at the farm. McKay's aunt and uncle allowed a menagerie of animals. What they didn't allow just seemed to show up. The peacocks were excellent watchdogs, and they sat perched across the top of the roofline of the farmhouse called "Homeplace." Peacocks are one of my favorite birds, and McKay and I both enjoyed their colorful feathers. One year, the peacocks served as a motivator for my Christmas present. McKay saw a beautiful pin in the shape of a peacock, and that same pin is still one of my most prized material possessions.

Down the road a piece was a store that sold basic goods. Next to the store was a large pond-like area that was fenced in to hold the store owner's alligators. The store sold marshmallows that people would buy, and then they'd walk across the stretch between the store and the pond, stand on a catwalk, and feed the alligators marshmallows. I did this only once and was not at all taken with an alligator smacking on a marshmallow. McKay thought it was the neatest deal since Popsicles.

The water park was near the store, and McKay and his aunt spent many hours playing in the sun at the park. He once tried to build a raft for floating on the pond near her home. This was a real Tom Sawyer adventure for him even though he was not successful. Nearby, boats were offered for rent, so we once floated on the river in a canoe and took a picnic lunch.

Another treat for McKay was a trip to the fire-sale store. This store sold items that had been slightly damaged during a fire, and the prices and variety of items made the trip to the store feel like a treasure hunt. McKay's aunt would allow him to shop until he found something that was so pleasing that he was a very satisfied little boy. (He once brought home a big blow-up canoe. Carl and I spent a day with him at Lake Conroe letting him float around until he was happy and worn out with the canoe.)

The fire-sale store and dollar stores were convenient stops along the way in Mississippi. McKay would usually find a shopping bag full of "stuff" for him to create something. The bag seemed to contain an endless array of clay, glitter, glue, stickers, paper, scissors, and more. Once the aunt sent him a package through the mail, and she enclosed goodies from the dollar store and the fire-sale store. She is a haphazard wrapper, and the package developed a hole in its side while in route to Texas. The lid to the glitter came off, and when the package arrived, glitter was trickling out of the opening. McKay asked if there was glitter from Mississippi to Texas. I laughed, but I also knew it was quite possible.

On one trip to the aunt's, a rooster was the latest arrival to the farm. McKay had not experienced a rooster before, so he would chase it and it would chase him. He became so aggravated once that he went into the house and said, "Me and that rooster are going to have us a little talk." When Carl and I met the aunt along the road so we could pick up McKay, we noticed right away a laundry basket and a cardboard box sitting at their feet. McKay's aunt had purchased him a baby rabbit and a rooster. The rooster was in the box, and the rabbit was in the laundry basket.

I rode eight hours—from Mississippi to Texas—in the backseat of the car with the rooster and the bunny. The box lid was closed, and the rooster was crowing. I knew he was cramped, but there really wasn't much I could do about it, short of putting him out by the side of the road, and that was unthinkable.

When we arrived home, we had no place for the bunny or the rooster. A quick trip to the hardware store yielded nails, fencing, and hinges for a door for the bunny cage. Carl and McKay built a cage on legs for the rabbit and a fenced area for the rooster. Everybody had a home.

The rabbit's name was Beatrice, and the rooster's name was Red on the Head. Beatrice grew to be a very big rabbit. Red crowed in the morning as the sun rose and almost every time a car drove by—in fact, he crowed any time he pleased. We had neighbors close by, and the restrictions were that dogs and cats were acceptable, as was one horse per acre. All other animals were to be projects for the county fair. The rooster and the bunny were not fair projects, so we were in a quandary as to what to do. We thought of the local petting zoo, so we called and they told us they were open to accepting animals from the county fair when the owners did not want to send them to the processing plants. McKay and I took a trip to the farm and discussed with them the possibility of taking Beatrice and Red. They agreed, with the stipulation that we would help them raise rabbits. We would take some baby rabbits and keep them to adult age, then return them and pick up more babies.

We took three miniature bunnies. Somehow, we did not quite figure out the swap of two for three. McKay named the adorable bunnies Martin, Coretta, and Selena. Beatrice and Red were left at the petting zoo, where they made numerous trips to exhibitions. Red stayed in the back pasture of the petting zoo and sometimes rode on the back of one of the cows. After Red and Beatrice were in their new home, the neighbors asked what had happened to the rooster. They told us they missed the crowing.

Our pets came and went; most lived to old age. Each entrance into our lives was as touching as each exit. Each new animal brought a series of memories that still leave me enriched, even after many years. I miss them and the moments of enjoying the velvet touch of the old snout of the golden retrievers. I miss the serenity the peaceful animals brought.

Chapter Two: My Greatest Prize

Carl regularly took McKay to the feed store, which may have seemed an odd place for a child, but he usually came home with something fun. Baby ducklings were the prize after one trip. The babies lived outside the back door in a cage for weeks. They were so cute, but so messy! The day came when Carl and McKay decided to release them into the wild: the pond on the public golf course down the street from the house. Carl and McKay put the babies down at the edge of the water, and then they ran, but the babies ran after them. Carl and McKay tried and tried to run fast enough to get away from the babies, but they could not. After a couple of days, I loaded the babies in a cardboard box and tipped the box in the edge of the water. While they couldn't see me because of the box, I ran home. After a while we took bread to the pond, and the babies were already happily enjoying their new surroundings.

The array of pets that McKay found and kept could fill many pages. When he was born, there were two dogs, Buffy and Boatswain. On a road trip, McKay fell over Boatswain, and she bit his mouth, causing the need for several stitches. We went to the nearest emergency room to have McKay examined, and the doctors and nurses in the emergency room were concerned that Carl or I had hit McKay. They went to the vehicle we were driving to make sure a dog was inside. When we arrived home, I rocked McKay and cried. He looked at me and said, "Woman, don't cry for me." Buffy and Boatswain died before McKay started school. We had what seemed like a never-ending series of cats. We seemed to lose cats either to death or by their wandering off. One Christmas we had no cats because of many losses, so Carl purchased a whatnot of two cats for McKay and me. He said maybe we could hold on to these for a while because these cats wouldn't die.

After old Buffy died, McKay once came to me and told me his dad was in the den crying again about Buffy. This had gone on for months, so I made the decision to begin the search for a golden retriever. I located a litter of puppies, and we made haste and picked out the largest puppy. The puppy was so fat her stomach drug the ground. We were elated, and we named her Buffy. She helped fill the empty spot in our hearts after Old Buffy's death.

After Boatswain's death, we were approached by our veterinarian about another golden retriever that was the golf course dog in a local neighborhood. My sister wanted a golden retriever, so we decided we would look at the dog for her. We took one look at Penny and made the decision that my sister couldn't have her: she had a home with us.

Cats came and went, but when we moved to our home named Mandala, we built an indoor/outdoor cattery that had A/C and heat. The dogs also had the same. The three cats that stayed lived until old age. Prior to the cattery, we had a cat named Axle Rod given to us. The first name we gave the cat came and went when she acquired the name Axle Rod after her trip to the restaurant with us one evening . . . she sat under the moving truck somewhere! McKay decided she probably rode on the axle, so her new name stuck.

Axle was not a friendly cat. I had to board an airplane after trying to catch Axle and get him into his plane carrier, and I spent most of the flight rubbing Neosporin into the scratches she had left on my arms as she fought the carrier. I had to take her to the vet to be cared for while we were out of town. One Sunday when Carl went to feed the "herd," he came home with some startling news: Axle had died during the night. We decided to wait to tell McKay until after church. When we arrived home from church, I asked Carl where he had placed Axle. He said, "In the trash can." I was infuriated with him and told him to get the cat out of the trash can because that would not only upset me, but also McKay. Carl wrapped Axle in a clean towel, and we told McKay that his dad had found him dead. McKay held the cat and rocked him, then gently kissed the dead cat on the head. He made some comment about this being the only time he was able to hold Axle. McKay gathered his friends for a funeral, and they dug a hole in the side flower bed next to the back door. He spoke a few words, and then informed his friends he was supposed to say the benediction.

There were three other cats. Tigger was a Christmas kitty we found in the house of a woman with a huge Christmas tree. We took McKay to see the kitten, but the tree was so big, we couldn't see the little cats. The lady pointed towards the tree and McKay dived in. Kittens scurried left and right, and McKay chose a yellow tabby whom he named Tigger.

Pepper, the next cat, was called a Texas Big, and he *was* big. He had a wonderful disposition, and from the time McKay was in first grade through the time he was in sixth, I carried Pepper to school for story time at least once a year. He would sit on my lap and look around the room and at the children. Usually, he would roll over on his back and hang his head off my knees to look at the boys and girls upside down. They were smitten with Pepper. During McKay's sixth grade year, I was asked if I would teach art for one day. I agreed if I could have a live model: I chose to take Pepper. Many of the boys and girls had been with Pepper since first grade, and they knew him, but the art teacher was amused at the number of children who entered the room and called Pepper by name. I told the classes that Pepper would not be with them in seventh grade, and we talked about their growing up and about Pepper's growing old. During art class, we closed the door, so Pepper was free to roam about the room. We placed the desks in groups of four so that the classes could have a place for Pepper to perch. He moved around the room and hopped on the desks as he looked at the art work. He eventually laid down on someone's paper and rolled on his back. The lesson for the day—draw and enjoy Pepper. By the end of the day, Pepper's hair looked like a piece of worn-out squirrel fur. The children had patted and rubbed and twisted little pieces of hair into points. He was a sight to behold. Of all his trips to school, it was his finest hour.

Frosty Ho Ho was another Christmas kitten. He was a white Himalayan with a smushed face and bright blue eyes. I should have said no to this little white one when I saw the breeder washing the kitty's face and cleaning his eyes. It did not dawn on me until later that the kitten did not have enough instinct to clean himself. Well, he didn't then, and he didn't for years to come, but it didn't matter to McKay; he was in love with the little ball of fur that looked as if he had stuck his tail in an electrical socket.

Out of nowhere, in 1990, a Brittany spaniel with a poor coat, protruding ribs, and horrible teeth showed up. A family friend named Ric and McKay thought he was just grand. Ric assured me that if the dog were groomed and neutered, he would give him to his father for Father's Day. It sounded like a good deal—help a dog in need and provide a Father's Day gift for a friend's dad. I opened the door to my Cadillac, and the dog hopped in and sat in a most dignified manner . . . considering his physical condition. We all agreed his name should be Fleetwood Cadillac Everett.

That night McKay telephoned his dad, who was out of town working. McKay gently made mention of the dog that had appeared and been given a name. Carl told McKay we should take the dog to the vet and McKay said, "We already have." He assured his dad that we had a home for Fleetwood, and his stay with us would only be until Father's Day.

The trip to the vet proved to be eventful. Fleetwood was neutered, groomed, and had his teeth cleaned. The receptionist shook a medicine bottle at us and it sounded like a baby rattler. The bottle contained the teeth that had to be pulled due to abscess. The vet informed us that Fleetwood would have died within a week from malnutrition if we had not rendered aid.

One day, McKay decided to send First Lady Barbara Bush's dog, Millie, a letter. We made our own stationery with paw prints. Millie responded with a postcard and a picture of herself and Mrs. Bush. McKay laughed, and talked to Fleetwood over and over about his mail from the White House dog.

Carl was able to sit still for longer periods of time than I, so he had the responsibility and privilege of watching every one of McKay's football practices. McKay had not wanted to play contact sports until seventh grade, and Carl had played football during high school, so he understood McKay's desire to do something in the sports arena.

Carl was open to doing activities with McKay at school. He built a rocket ship with McKay and they launched it from the school grounds. The children in McKay's class were in awe, and the rocket launch prompted a summer trip for Carl and McKay to Space Camp.

One of the many fun summer times was during vacation Bible school. I was usually McKay's teacher, along with several of my friends who all tried to make VBS fun and memorable. We made stained-glass windows from waxed paper, crayon chips, and a hot iron. Carl cut pieces for a birdhouse for each child, and they laboriously nailed the houses together by pounding and pounding with the hammers. (We were told we were a distraction to the other classes because our projects were too much fun.) The kids painted the houses and took them home, and I am reminded of the birdhouses to this day when I see birds. The children may not remember everything from VBS, but I'm sure they remembered the birdhouses!

We made several local moves during McKay's life because as part of our business strategy, we would sell a home and then rent a new one while we built again. With all of this moving, two incidents remain strong memories for me. In one place we lived, the neighborhood had many houses. As soon as we had unloaded the boxes and furniture into the house, McKay told us he was going to meet the neighbors. Mrs. Wong, the next-door neighbor McKay had gone to meet, told me later that on that day, he had knocked on her door and asked if she had any children his age. She told him that all her children were grown. She said he stood a while, looked at her with a puzzled gaze, and asked, "Mrs. Wong, did you know you are Oriental?" She said she told him yes, she knew she was Oriental.

Mrs. Wong was a wonderful neighbor. In her backyard, she had a garden that was visible from one of the windows where McKay liked to curl up and observe the world. He watched her as she gardened some most unusual plants, things like the loofah sponges that grew on the garden gate. Once McKay yelled out for me to come and look at the Mrs. Wong's persimmon tree. It looked so strange that we walked next door and asked Mrs. Wong what was going on. She told us she was trying to save the persimmons for Mr. Wong, and the birds loved the persimmons, so she had dressed each piece of fruit in a scrap of panty hose.

While we were renting another home, McKay was a preschooler. He was intrigued with buried treasure and treasure maps. One summer day, I had heard so much talk of treasure, I asked Carl if he would watch McKay long enough for me to burn the edges of some paper, draw a treasure map, go to town to purchase some cheap dollar store stuff that could pass as treasure, dig a hole, and bury the treasure. He agreed. McKay was beyond excitement when he stumbled on the map and realized the treasure was so close to home. He grabbed the shovel and began to dig. As he dug up the pieces of treasure, he remarked that it really wasn't treasure because it was plastic. Oh, well.

Dancing was one of the thousands of fun times McKay and I had together. When he was small, he would wear his socks and slide and moonwalk through the house. We would jitterbug and laugh and dance until we were tired. Each day, he would turn on some fifties music, grab me, and say, "Let's dance!" When times called for quieter music, he would listen to classical. Music and dance were a part of our daily lives.

Our fun times were a source of rebirth for me; the renewal of the child in me, and the freshness of a relationship between a mother and her son surpassed anything I had ever known. The times of running through the house and hiding from him and then jumping out and yelling "gotcha," and the times I watched the soles of his feet and the back of his head as he ran from me left me with priceless snapshots that are always in my heart. Walking, resting in rocking chairs, riding bicycles while looking for pennies, and just plain living life . . . we had a simple life in which childhood was respected as a vital part of life and growing. Since during my own early years, I had endured so many highs and lows, the child part of me was most affected. Spending fun times with McKay as he grew helped heal that sad child in me.

McKay blazed many trails through the local woods. He would find railroad spikes, rocks, or anything that he could call important or create a story around. The last outing we took together began on our bicycles, as we both had a love for our bikes. We pedaled with him leading the way to an opening in the woods, where we left our bikes and proceeded on foot. He took me to his special places and shared with me the adventures he had had in the woods around White Oak Creek. On the way out of the woods, as he was holding a branch, he accidentally let it go too soon, and it hit me in the face and scratched my eye. It took a trip to the eye doctor to determine if there was any damage to my eye, and thankfully there wasn't. Dr. Avery asked what I had been doing, and since McKay had come with me to the doctor, he began to share what had happened. Dr. Avery only smiled as McKay relayed the events.

One of the outdoor toys McKay enjoyed the most was the skateboard he got when he was older and could maneuver by himself. He became so proficient at skateboarding that he would leash Penny, his golden retriever, and allow her to pull him up and down the roads of the neighborhood. Penny was gentle, yet playful in nature. She loved her times with McKay and the skateboard. While I worked in the yard, I would have brief glimpses of them both as they passed the house . . . McKay yelling hello and Penny giving a bark.

One summer day, we decided to ride our bikes after we washed the car, which we had left in the driveway. Carl had a new bike that was good for trail riding, and why I decided to ride his bike is still a mystery to me. I was too short for his bike, but I thought it would be fun, so I got on it as best I could, and it began to roll. The next thing I heard was a thud, then breaking glass. I had flipped and landed on top of the trunk of my car. McKay ran over and sized up the situation. He told me there was no blood, and he helped me get down. He told me we would start over, but this time on my own bike. His kindness and ability to take control in a situation like that left me feeling confident that he was maturing in a positive way.

Holiday times were very special in our home, and each new holiday brought a new opportunity for wonderful memories. On Valentine's Day, there was the Love Bug who would deliver "stuff" to McKay. Most of the stuff was from the local dollar store. Nothing special or expensive, just an opportunity to say "I Love You." Easter—with the Easter Bunny—was a great time for me to enjoy my collection of rabbit stuff. Before Easter one year, we spent some time in the barn building yard art that we could stick in the ground. We cut out rabbits and painted them. There was a dogwood tree near the road, and we purchased cheap, colorful, plastic eggs and put them on the tree. We once made a wreath of silk flowers for the back door, but we had to move it because it was so realistic, it fooled the bees, and they made it a risky endeavor trying to go into the house.

The Fourth of July meant flags and a bonfire with marshmallows and hot dogs. It meant that McKay would beat on his drums and salute, and he would ask if we knew any war stories. When he went to Washington DC, he had visited the Vietnam Memorial and had done a rubbing of the name of a relative who had died. He liked to hear stories of America and the struggles and battles that were fought to bring us to where we are today.

Halloween meant a visit to the grocery store to pick out pumpkins for the front porch. Some were decorated with markers, some were carved with a knife and filled with flashlights. Our front porch was a clutter of pumpkins. When McKay was very young, we would attend the Fall Festival at church instead of trick-or-treating. He so badly wanted to win the contest for the best costume. He would plan and plan, but it wasn't until he came up with the idea of a family costume that he won first place. We visited a costume store in New Orleans, and McKay was inspired to do a "family costume." He found a small, green tortoise costume, and after that, it was a year-long project of piecing together the other characters. I was the hare, and his dad was the flag man. McKay's costume was easiest. Mine was next in line in difficulty, and then his dad's was the most time-consuming to make.

McKay's local grandmother, Raleigh Mae, made my costume out of white, furry fabric. It was a job to just live in the same room with the sewing machine while she was making the costume. White hairs would linger in the air. I found some bunny ears and decided to carry a real bunch of carrots with the green tops still attached. Carl's costume required some searching for a striped shirt and some material to make the racing flags, but by the time October rolled around, the costumes were ready, and we had kept a tight lid on our year-long endeavor. We had planned our entrance into the church activity building, and even the minor details like green glitter freckles on McKay were not overlooked. He won! He crawled on his hands and knees and wagged the little piece of a tail that was on the costume. We all had a great time.

Other costumes McKay created were great, too. He was a groundhog in one school play. The suit took an afternoon in the fabric store and more time with the seamstress. I had a machine, but I spent more time ripping out than sewing up. The year he decided to be Dick Tracy was the most costly. We shopped for fabric and a pattern, and we had to make several trips to different stores to find a hat that *almost* fit. We purchased two cans of bright yellow spray paint so we could paint the hat, but the first can barely gave a hint of yellow to the felt hat. The paint seemed to disappear as soon as it hit the fabric. The second can didn't do much more. In all, we used almost six cans of spray paint to make the Dick Tracy hat yellow.

Tarzan, Indiana Jones, Dick Tracy, and Superman were frequent visitors to our home. Each came and went with his own lines from movies and with his own costume. The character that McKay seemed to enjoy most came when he was in fourth grade. It was a tradition in the elementary school he attended for the fourth graders to perform *The Nutcracker*. When McKay was five years old, we took him to Houston to the ballet performance of *The Nutcracker*, but about three quarters of the way through the performance, he became bored and decided he was ready to leave. In fourth grade, he remembered enough of the ballet to tell us he wanted a very important part, but one that required no line memorization. He tried out for and got the part of the Rat King. He practiced and practiced his sword fighting, which seemed to be the most important part of the role as Rat King. Thank goodness the school supplied the costume. I had helped build and add to the existing costumes that had been collected over the years for Christmas performances, so the biggest jobs

I had that year were the whiskers and nose McKay wanted painted on his face. The performance was a hit, and his sword fighting was superb.

We usually spent Thanksgiving in Mississippi because Carl and I wanted to reserve Christmas as a time to establish family traditions. In November, we would spend several nights with my mother, who would prepare a large dinner and decorate the house for Christmas. McKay was always so excited that he was having Christmas early. He would enter the house with his eyes as bright as the Christmas tree. The family would gather, and since there was a long stretch of time between births of grandchildren—and McKay was the youngest for now—the focus was on him. We would sit and watch McKay open gifts and applaud as he demonstrated or modeled each gift.

One holiday season, the men purchased fireworks. Carl, McKay, and my brother Paul went outside to light up the sky. Fireworks are not of interest to me so I stayed inside visiting. McKay ran through the door smelling of smoke and with a frightened look in his eyes. He said he was not supposed to tell us, but the field was on fire. We dashed outside and the sky was lit up—but not from fireworks. The flames were coming from a brush fire that had been started by the fireworks. Carl and Paul were beating the flames with large branches from a tree. They didn't want us to see what they had done, so they yelled for us to go back inside. They did control the fire and finally put it out, but not without some moments of great concern that it might reach the neighbor's home. They were tired and sooty by the time the fire was out, and the holiday fireworks were put away for the rest of the season.

Christmas was one of our favorite times together. We would purchase a tall tree, and place it in the entryway of our home. One tradition that developed was that the trees became the bearer of memories, memories mostly centered around our life with McKay. There were ornaments given to me by students of years past. Other ornaments were from friends and family. When McKay was born, I began placing items on the tree that would stir the leaves of memory in my mind. I kept items from flower arrangements I received when McKay was born. There was a little rocking horse with blue plastic wording that said, "It's

A Boy." A piano ornament, lots of angels, my mother's twelve-disciple bracelet, Carl's mother's eyeglasses, a music box from Mattie Lou, a bell from my Aunt Lavone, and Mama Lee's hanky all had their rightful place on the memory tree. The tree invoked laughter, tears, and talk between McKay and me about times he did not remember. When he helped decorate, the tree would be bottom heavy because the ornaments were hung where he could reach.

McKay had his own little tree for his room. About five feet high and skinny, the tree begged for decoration. One year in November, McKay spent most of one night in the attic *dragging* out Christmas goodies . . . I mean dragging the stuff from the attic to his bedroom. It was the biggest mess he had ever made. The next morning while I cleaned, he was asleep in his room with the tree lights on and his snoring Santa plugged in and operational. I ended up spending the better part of that day cleaning up the mess. From that day on, we did not undecorate McKay's tree. Carl would walk it to the attic as it was decorated and walk it out the next year.

Each year, we spent time reading the Christmas story in the Bible. McKay had a keen interest of what Jesus's life was like when he was a child. He wanted to know what He did to stay busy and what He did at Christmastime. McKay and I visited a book store to find some books we could read in order to satisfy his curiosity. He also wanted a menorah, so we purchased one when McKay was six. We read the books each year and lit the candles, and it seemed to give McKay a deeper meaning of Christmas.

When McKay was eleven, he received a telescope for Christmas. He was a stargazer, and when he got the telescope, he was so excited he put it together right away. As he was going out the door, he tripped and fell, breaking the lens. He still gazed in awe at the Heavens, even through the broken lens.

McKay's birthday was always a special event. Not just for the three of us, but for friends and family. Many members of our families had thought that Carl and I would not have any children because the years had rocked along without any. McKay was the first grandchild in years in my family, so he was always made to feel special during his birthday. One year, he had a skating party, and family members drove from Mississippi to be with him. The fondest memory of this party is the video: Carl forgot to turn off the camera, so we have a nice view of the wall at the skating rink intermingled with skating feet and an occasional view of a child skating in the distance.

McKay once requested an adult birthday party, and I wondered what he meant by this description. We went to the party store, and he strolled through the different party themes and decided on a Hawaiian party. I soon found myself renting the pool at the YMCA and having a cake baked with a scene from Hawaii on the icing. The party treats were goggles and flippers for the boys and grass skirts for the girls. He had a grand time, but I do remember thinking that the next party would be on a budget.

One year, McKay was quieter than usual when his birthday rolled around. He asked if just family could get together and go to dinner. This was not the norm, but we agreed if that was what he wanted to do. Carl, McKay, McKay's Uncle Paul, and I made dinner plans at a local restaurant. Carl and I planned a surprise for McKay. We purchased an extra-large, overstuffed bear that was about four feet tall. We told McKay that a special guest would be joining us. He did not know who the guest was until he walked in the restaurant, and the bear was sitting at a table waiting for him. He was so surprised. As he got older, the birthday scene changed from juvenile to teenaged, and he requested the usual pizza and friends. There was a moment or two of grief when I realized that McKay was growing up. With each new stage, I grieved the loss of the former stage of McKay's life.

McKay's friends were varied in gender, personality, and interests, and our neighborhood was a great resource for finding friends. One girl, Lauren, lived only a short walk down the road or through the woods. She was as adventuresome as McKay. One summer afternoon, McKay rode by the back window on his bike. He was wearing a crash helmet, and Lauren was wearing a crash helmet. She was riding in his wagon, which was tied to his bike. I realized then and there she truly had a love for McKay. Why else would she wear a crash helmet and ride in the wagon? As the years passed, she became less and less of an adventuresome tomboy and more and more a real live girl. McKay was totally taken aback when she had her ears pierced and wore hoop earrings. He came through the back door in a flurry and exclaimed he did not understand why she would get hoops.

The home next door had three children: Heather, Cody, and Liz. The two youngest played regularly with McKay. They biked, hiked, swam, and role played. They once staged a wedding.

One neighbor, Zak, was McKay's age. McKay and Zak would sleep over at each other's homes. One night when Zak was at our home, they played in the walk-in attic. They decided to create a spaceship, so they emptied a cardboard box that contained tax returns and receipts. They unpacked Christmas decorations and used the beads to create the flashing lights on the spaceship box. They must have become bored because they even played barbershop. When Zak arrived home the next day, his mom called and asked if I liked McKay's haircut. They had cut each other's hair. When Zak's family moved into the neighborhood, McKay was enjoying his microphone and speaker. He had opened one of the windows of the second story and was singing at the top of his lungs. Zak's family still remembers hearing McKay's voice throughout the neighborhood.

Two friends, Trent and Angela, who were brother and sister, enjoyed playing with McKay when it could be a twosome. The three of them together were certainly a crowd. McKay enjoyed their home, and when I had gone my limit with McKay, I would ask if he could play with them for a while. There was a level of activity in their home that he did not have in ours because he had no siblings. To observe sibling rivalry was entertainment to McKay. He once met Angela at the movies and repeatedly said, "This is not a date! This is not a date!" to the ticket sales lady.

McKay had two friends in middle school: Bud and Chad. Both guys were in our home regularly. They romped in the woods, played games, rode bikes, and played video games. One of the studious guys helped McKay remain more focused in school. The other friend was fun loving, and between the two friends, they provided a great balance for McKay.

During his times at summer camps, McKay always came home with a long list of names, phone numbers, and addresses. He was diligent about keeping in touch with family and friends.

At bedtime, McKay would ask for his music so he could sleep. He liked classical until one day when a friend of mine left a music book on the back porch. The piano book contained beautiful music that caught McKay's attention when I began practicing. He told me that the new music could be his music to sleep by. Most nights, I would play the piano as he drifted off to sleep. He would say, "Please, play my music so I can sleep." His favorite was "Surely the Presence." After a while, I would go upstairs and stroke McKay's hair as he slept. The quietness of the house allowed me to hear his breathing. I remember the times as if they were yesterday, and yet they were long, long ago. These are the moments when a mom wishes she could stop the clock or bottle the memory.

Music was a part of our daily lives. He heard the song "Memory" from the Broadway production of CATS. When the production arrived in Houston, he was determined to go. The song "Memory" seemed to stick with the both of us. It was a point of bonding that I did not understand. I purchased the sound track, and we listened over and over to the music. We would lie on the floor in my bathroom, turn on the foot warmers, and listen to our favorite music.

Sometimes when McKay played the piano, he would compose his own songs. Carl and I would ask him to play something soft that brought out soft feelings. Sometimes we would ask if he could play something exciting or a piece that sounded like a struggle or a war. I could ask him how he was feeling, and he could play his feelings on the piano. He had a great love for music, and that love helped fill our home with many hours of wonderful sounds.

When McKay was born, the snapshots began. We took pictures and had pictures taken often. As soon as he was able to look through the lens of a camera and press the button, he began taking photos himself. I am not suggesting that he always took identifiable pictures, but he had fun. When McKay was around the age of four, I took him to a local photographer to have Christmas photos made of the two of us. As I pulled in the parking space, he began to verbally give excuses as to why he did not want to sit for a photo. I knew the pictures would probably be poor if his attitude didn't turn around. I told him that we would give the photos to his dad for Christmas. That was enough motivation for him to cooperate through the two sittings. I told him what he was doing was really important.

On Christmas day, he gave his dad the photos. He put one arm around Carl's neck and one arm around mine and said, "Thank you for being such good parents." He was so proud of the photos. They are a storehouse of memories for me.

Through the years, McKay would draw us near by putting one arm around me and one around Carl. About age eleven, he began saying, "How about those Lions?" He had watched a TV program or had heard these words somewhere, and they stuck. He was getting to an age where he did not want to hugged or kissed in public, so he told us that if he said those words, they meant, "I love you."

Of course, McKay had some disappointments in his life. They not only tore at him—they tore at me, knowing that I could not protect him from the pains of growing up and experiencing real life. The times I saw him dip to a low were when a girl only wanted to be a friend, not a girlfriend. Once, I watched from the sidelines as he wrestled with the news, and even though he was only in fourth grade, he had the maturity to call her after much soul wrestling and say, "Can we at least be friends?"

I watched as he became pulled by comments from a group of kids who did not like one of his other friends. I silently cheered as he stood firm and continued to befriend the boy even when it was not the popular thing to do at the time. He did not understand the group's ridicule of another child who was a really neat person.

I saw how he dealt with the comments and concerns we discussed about our adult friends who were struggling with issues in life. With childlike faith, McKay would say they only needed to go to church and know Jesus.

I wanted to help but I had to let him discover his own way to learn certain things in school. McKay reversed letters, numbers, and words until fourth grade, which made schoolwork an extra effort for him. He had to work hard to compensate for this problem, but overcame it with determination and a decision to persist.

I stood proudly as I watched and listened as he stood his ground once with an older child. After a quick scuffle on the back porch, McKay came inside he said, "If you can't beat 'em, eat 'em! Don't worry, I know about AIDS. I bit him through his pants leg." He was so frustrated that he had to stand up to someone larger.

Each child on this earth is unique, and their idiosyncrasies distinguish them from all others. One characteristic behavior of McKay's was his sleep habit. He did not require much sleep, and what little sleep he got was sometimes in his bed, but most often at the foot of mom and dad's bed, on the floor in a sleeping bag, in the closet in our room, or on a pallet on the floor. The closet, being my "safe" place from childhood, had been legitimized in the last home. I hung draperies over the clothes, and installed a padded bench that was the length of my body. Even I slept there when I needed time alone or time in what I considered a safe place. This was certainly a carryover from my childhood.

I look back with definite recollection of McKay's beginnings with God. He always broke the word amen into two special words: "A MEN." Another time, our cat was missing for only a few hours, but McKay sat on the back steps praying aloud for his cat to come home. I sat with him, wondering if the cat were in the edge of the woods, listening to McKay. I was with him when the cat nonchalantly strolled up the hill and rested at our feet. The look in McKay's eyes said, *I believe!*

Chapter Two: My Greatest Prize

In Conroe, when we attended church, we sat very near the front. To keep McKay busy and quiet, I carried pencils, paper, and crayons. He would draw the choir director, the choir, and individual choir members—all of their mouths looked like the letter O. If he got restless, I would draw faces on the interior tips of my fingers, and we would have a puppet show.

Another treat at church was the every-summer vacation Bible school. McKay sang in the choir group, and one evening, they held a program in the gymnasium. The director used risers for the children to stand on, and McKay was on the top back row. We were enjoying the program and watching McKay sing when we noticed that he became engrossed with a button on the wall. He pointed his index finger to press the button. All the while, Carl and I were trying to get his attention with hand and head motions and soft shouts of *no!* We did not succeed. McKay pressed the button and a movie screen lowered behind the children. The choir director ran to the button and pressed it, and the screen rose again. The program continued as if nothing had happened, but it was a tense moment.

McKay was a bundle of questions concerning the Bible, but we, as his parents, couldn't answer most of them. I had planned to save my library of religious books for McKay, and I hoped to one day pass my Bible to him. I have a special Bible that Carl received on his thirtieth birthday, His friend Bill gave it to him inscribed with the verse from John 15:13: "Greater love hath no man than to lay down his life for his friend."

Before McKay was born, I began reading this Bible. After his birth, I wrote sermon notes in the margins as I read. For a period of time, I wrote notes to McKay, and it was my intention to read the Bible until it was worn out, then to pack it away for McKay to have as an adult or upon my death. I couldn't wait for him to become an adult to read the notes, so when I wrote to him while we sat in church, I would nudge him and let him read my scribbles so he'd know my thoughts and feelings about him. I have tried to retire this Bible and get a new one, but I can't. The love I have for this book is beyond reason, and even though it is worn and torn and held together by tape, it is one of my most valued possessions. In the Bible, McKay would have found notes from me and from friends and acquaintances, a picture of a child with cancer, and notations where prayers had been answered.

I was reared Presbyterian; Carl was reared Baptist. I felt strongly about parents dedicating their children to God, and it really concerned me that I didn't drive McKay by the Presbyterian church and have him christened—with or without Carl. One afternoon when McKay was a few months old, my cousin Cheryl paid McKay and me an unexpected visit. She told me she had come to dedicate McKay, and I was touched by her sensitivity; she hadn't even known that I longed to dedicate McKay.

McKay grew up knowing that I believed in prayer. I may have been naive, but I was a believer nonetheless. Twice, McKay witnessed two children being touched by the sincere prayers of loving people. The Christmas we took him to New York was one of those times. A few days before we left for New York, it was raining and storming. I received a phone call from an older friend in Mississippi. She relayed a story to me about a Texas child born with cancer eleven or so years ago. The cancer had gone into remission, and the mother had moved the child to Mississippi to what she thought would be life at a slower pace, with cleaner air and family she could get to know. Small world—when they moved to Mississippi, they moved to my hometown, Magee, and rented an apartment from a dear friend. My former hairdresser was the child's Sunday school teacher, and a relative of Mattie Lou's was the preacher at the small church that the family with the sick child attended. My friend's request was simple: she asked if I knew anyone who would go to Houston and pray for this child. The cancer was no longer in remission, and the family had returned to Houston, expecting the child to die by year's end.

The weather was so bad I didn't have the heart to ask someone else to go, especially during the holidays. Carl said he would take me, and McKay went with us. I really didn't know what to do or say since I'd not done this before, but I knew I had to try.

Chapter Two: My Greatest Prize

When we arrived at the dark and quiet house, we were greeted by the mother. The frail, weak child sat in the living room. No one had to tell her she was dying. We all talked for a while, and I felt overwhelmed, because so far in my life, I had managed to avoid facing death. I even had Carl take our old pets to the veterinarian because I couldn't watch them be put down. The sight of this turbaned child, Kathy, wrenched my heart in many directions. We asked her what she would like from New York for Christmas, and she told us, "Minnie Mouse." I told Kathy that a friend of ours had asked me to come pray, and I hoped this little girl and her family were glad we were there. I don't remember what I said, but I know I spoke from my heart. When we returned to the car, Carl told me that if he were ever sick, he would want me to pray like that for him.

This little sick girl touched our family deeply. I can neither write not speak words that fully portray the impact she had on our lives. I still get teary eyed when I think of her and her struggle, and I'm grateful McKay was able to experience so much by being a part of her life.

We bought her the Minnie Mouse in New York and delivered it to her when we returned to Texas. Kathy's mother called to say thank you, and relayed to us that her daughter wanted to get better so she could visit our church. She did live—both mother and daughter spent the weekend in our home and attended church one Sunday. Kathy felt so at ease in our home that she removed her turban.

As I watched Kathy and McKay play and talk, it reminded me not to forsake the child side of me—the sensitive side, the side willing to open up and be free to express feelings. I had such respect for McKay as he opened his part of our home to Kathy. Later, we sent a package to Kathy. Her mother told us that when she lay the present on her daughter's lap, the little girl said she knew it was a Precious Moments Bible. She was right. There was an "in-touchness" that defies logical explanation between our family and this child.

The ups and downs and highs and lows of the emotional waves crashing on shore left us forever touched by Kathy. The reality of children suffering and dying brought my life with Carl and McKay into clearer focus, and I began to value health and life more and more in my daily life. I attribute many positives to this child who suffered and who allowed me in for a period of time. I will be forever touched.

The other time McKay witnessed a child's being touched by prayer was when we heard of a teenager who suffered from a head injury from a car accident. McKay watched from afar during this time, as the child was not expected to live. Carl and I went to the hospital to visit the parents, despite my fear of spinal meningitis (a classmate in high school had died from this illness, and I had since been afraid of hospitals). When Carl and I arrived, we were told by the medical staff that the boy was suspected of having spinal meningitis, and I was almost immobilized with fear. I went with the stepfather to the ICU to pray. I had never seen someone dying before and his matted eyes were terrifying. In my ignorance, I told God I would be there for these parents and this child if He would only watch after McKay and keep him safe. Months later, a handsome teenager sat behind me in church. He in no way resembled the person in ICU.

There are also those who touched McKay's life in simple but profound ways. Mr. Webb taught Sunday school to McKay when he was a toddler. Around the age of ten, McKay took notice of Mr. Webb's garden when we passed by one summer afternoon. The garden was full of assorted plants, but the big sunflower blooms are what caught McKay's eye. He was mesmerized by the towering bursts of yellow. McKay wanted to help Mr. Webb plant sunflowers, so the next summer, I asked Mr. Webb if McKay could help him plant. He agreed, and they made plans. Mr. Webb allowed McKay to experience the whole "inchtalada" (his word for enchilada when he was in second grade). He hoed, he pulled weeds, he mounded the dirt, he watered the ground, and he got frustrated and eyeballed me plenty because he was not fond of manual labor. He finally got to plant the seeds. They grew, they bloomed, they died—and McKay was a part of the experience! Two years ago, Mr. Webb called and asked me to come pick sunflowers—the first batch since McKay's death.

Carl spent some evenings tucking McKay into bed; I filled in when he was out of town, and sometimes we did it together. One evening, Carl came down the steps and said McKay had told him he believed in God and knew he had a need for Him in his life, but he wasn't quite ready to join the church. Months later, on April 25, 1993, one day before my birthday, McKay leaned over and whispered, "I'm joining the church today. Don't tell Dad; he'll cry. Happy birthday, Mom. I love you." On May 16, 1993, McKay was baptized.

As I leave these pages, I feel as if I am saying goodbye to a best friend I have not visited in years. I have searched through boxes for every reminder of my friend, my son. I have looked at pictures, schoolwork, and visited with friends, family, and myself. I have allowed a gentle wind to blow the leaves of my mind, to stir the memories, to send some flying end over end until I remembered some of the sweet sounds and pictures stored in my heart forever.

McKay was the most important thing in Carl's and my marriage. I loved Carl, but the love from and for McKay struck a deeper chord within me, a chord I had never heard before I was McKay's mother. One of his teachers expressed it in writing with words that fit my feelings perfectly: "When I was with McKay, I felt I was in the presence of someone special. There was an effervescence about him."

I step back from my motherly feelings and look at his life in a moment of detachment. I ask myself, *Are not all children special?* I expect no answer to my own question because children have always played a major role in my life—from taking care of siblings, to teaching school, to parenting McKay. A writer once wrote of childhood and classified it in a manner that has repeatedly come to my mind: the "sanctity" of childhood is that period of time when all of us gain the foundation for much of life. It's the period of innocence when love and nurturing are the rich treasures in the life of a child.

How do I bring these pages to life? How do I make them breathe, speak, and tap dance in penny loafers? How do I make these words say, *I am McKay?*

McKay was my only son, my only child, my greatest prize.
McKay was a stargazer.
He received a telescope for Christmas.
He promptly put it together.
As he was going out the door, he tripped and fell.
He continued to gaze in awe, even through the broken lens.
—Paulette

Chapter Three
1990–1995

As if a song were ending during the years 1990–1995, the oil and gas market became slower and slower, and less and less of our income came from this area. Carl and I went on with life, even though our circumstances were changing. We did what oil and gas work came our way, we built a home for ourselves, and we opened a home-building company, joined Amway, and enjoyed the moments we had with McKay. Carl and I talked about the future, and we tried to plan fun things. If there was one area where Carl and I failed, however, it was that we put McKay first and did not keep our marriage stable and growing. Many parents make this common human error in judgment. The marriage continues to take nurturing and work in order to grow and prosper—with or without children.

Our two larger homes were built with the South in mind. Since two of the residence homes that we built were large, and their exterior designs and landscaping were reminiscent of the South, I thought it might be a good marketing tool to name them, as is tradition even today. We planted a weeping willow outside the master bathroom window, and friends would tease us and say that the bathroom looked as if it were situated on a bayou. Carl and I had visited the homes of the Old South in New Orleans and Atlanta, and had made several trips to Natchez, staying in two of its old homes. McKay was right at home exploring the homes and the well-kept grounds.

We had sold one home named Dunyana (Arabic for "our world"), then rented a home and built almost across the street from the home we had just sold. The new home was named *Mandala*. In a dream one night, I saw this home, and then my dream came true and the home was built.

This home ended up with the name Mandala—a word that had first appeared in my life in junior high. Pearl S. Buck wrote and titled a book that bears the name Mandala. I was spellbound by her writings, and the name stuck. Another time, a friend had given me the book *Josef the Baker*. In the book, Josef drew the Hebrew instrument, a mandala, in the fine dust of flour that settled on the tabletop. When searching for a name for our home, I thought of the recurring times this word had come into my life. I researched the meaning, and found that the dictionary defined it as the centering down of the soul, as the process of finding oneself, and as a Hindu symbol used in meditation. Since the house was to have a double spiral staircase, I thought of the stairwell to my soul. For years, I felt I did not really know myself. I didn't know what, if anything, I could make of my life that would be of lasting benefit. I knew I could try to pass on to McKay what I had learned from my grandmother and from life, but I felt a void when I searched for the purpose that I felt would bring a deeper peace inside me.

When Carl and I married, we did not fathom that we would have the opportunity to build two nice homes. He grew up in a 900-square-foot Jim Walter-type home on the chicken farm, and his bedroom was so small he could barely walk around the edge of the bed. I grew up in a series of homes. My parents built, sold, rented, and then repeated the process until they could build a home large enough for six children. The homes Carl and I built were used for living in and for entertaining, mostly for the church. Our homes were open and had lots of windows. I usually painted at the kitchen table since the light was so good there. One of our houses rested on three well-landscaped acres with over 500 azaleas. One year I thought so much about my Aunt Lavone and her yard that was filled with caladiums that I purchased 1000 caladium bulbs, and I planted every one of them. I got a little carried away, but it was the moment of a lifetime to see all of those caladiums waving to me when the wind blew.

McKay went through a phase of wanting to help with the yard. He had watched *Edward Scissorhands* and had nearly destroyed the magnolia trees I had given McKay and Carl one year for Easter. I could not believe the damage he did with a pair of lawn shears.

McKay grew up with experiences that ranged from living in a rental home to living in our own small home . . . and eventually into our own large ones. He was adaptable and could adjust easily to each new move.

When we moved into Mandala, McKay was a second grader. We had lived there for approximately six weeks, when Carl came home one day and told me of a conflict at work. I was standing at the island in the kitchen, and suddenly I heard a rustling sound behind my left shoulder. I turned around to look, but there wasn't anything there. My heart and stomach suddenly felt sick, and—I don't know how to say it other than spit it out—I felt as if angels were flying away. I told Carl I felt we needed to sell the home and move away, maybe even back to Mississippi. He became very frustrated with me and said the boxes were not all unpacked, and I was talking of moving again. The discussion ended.

In retrospect, I remember feeling alone during that period of my life. The angels that had been with me had flown away. Although in the past, I have had several experiences that left me very aware of my feelings and of the presence of God, I had not ever experienced any feelings such as these.

Once, one of our cats was shot by a neighbor. I was totally taken aback that someone would be so cruel. The veterinarian did what he could, but there was nerve damage. McKay and I would not give up; we prayed and we took that cat to the oriental acupuncture doctor for treatments. The doctor's office was lined with patients who were in physical pain—one lady even had a scarf around her head and face because she could not bear the wind to touch her skin. This was my first experience with people who were suffering from unstoppable pain. McKay and I would enter the office waiting room with the cat in a laundry basket. We would visit with people while we waited our turn. The little doctor looked at me one day and told me he would get McKay another cat. I knew then it was hopeless.

I prayed and prayed for God to show mercy to the cat. I was so naive. It was a time of slow acceptance for me, and it caused me to reflect on sick children and the parents who were at a loss as to what to do for their children. I cried not only for our cat—I cried for the sick and dying children whom I did not even know. My insides were in knots because the horizon only showed death for the cat. One night, after praying for God to show mercy, God spoke to me plainly in my heart. He said, "You learn mercy." Within a few days the cat had to be euthanized, an act of mercy.

At a restaurant once, Carl had handed me a Houston newspaper. The front page contained an article about a child who had died due to black pepper being poured down the child's throat. I was so overwrought by a child's death, even a child I didn't know, that I couldn't eat. When I returned home, I prayed, stomped my feet, and shook my fist at God. I demanded of God, "Why don't you get down off that throne and do something?" In my heart, a voice I know said, "I did." I can take you to the square of flooring where He stopped my demanding, stomping, and fist shaking.

During this time, Carl and I broke from our routine of building a home for ourselves. We tried our hand at building smaller homes, as Carl felt this would supply a need in our community. Basically, we built too nice a home for its size, so our profits were zip. In fact, I think we were in the negative. There were several times when we would give upgrades away so there would be more in the home for people to enjoy. One single mom whose husband had died needed a desk in her kitchen. She got the desk, a gift from us. Finally, Carl had to abandon his dream of providing well-built smaller homes.

Carl's best friend, who lived near us, worked in the oil patch when he could. I think he was feeling the crunch of finding less and less work, so he joined Amway. The enticement of income plus residuals from someone else's efforts drew his as well as Carl's interest. In the past, we had talked of selling our home, and Carl's friend called one Sunday afternoon to ask if he could bring someone to look at our home. He said the husband and wife were interested in purchasing a home in the area. The man and his wife came and viewed our home, and they pitched Amway the entire time. They had apparently made up their interest in purchasing the home as a way of gaining entrance into our lives. The point of vulnerability for me was when the couple said if we joined Amway, we could help others help themselves.

So Carl and I joined. The objective of Amway was to sign up friends, family, and business contacts who would purchase products from Amway. We would be paid a percentage based on the amount purchased by those we had enlisted. The positive aspect of Amway was meeting some neat people; the negative, in my opinion, is that the business painted illusions and mental pictures of grandiosity that caused reality to fade. Some of the illusions are achievable, but some could not be reached during the lifetime of six people. I think that when grandiosity takes over, the truth becomes clouded. Amway's most alluring sales pitch says that one will have less work and more money in Amway than in a present job. If we work the business now, we can reap the rewards later and retire early. I should have held onto the saying that I had repeated many times in our marriage: God intended for us to work.

McKay had reached the age where he was beginning to feel like he wanted to be independent, and he did not want a sitter. When Carl and I would go shopping or to a movie, we would call McKay every thirty minutes or so to check on him. When we went to Amway meetings, we allowed him to stay home alone, but we called often to check on him.

Carl had assumed the task of paying bills when I was pregnant with McKay and could not seem to subtract one from two. Since I didn't keep track of the money coming in and out, I couldn't trace all the dollars we invested in Amway, but my final guesstimation of money spent, including checks paid to us, was approximately $10,000 out of our personal funds. Needless to say, Amway wasn't working out quite like the storybook profile depicted.

I had learned the value of saving money when I was younger; my sister had once developed a serious brain infection, and I had watched as her illness set my parents back financially. I recall my mother and dad doing things I never dreamed they would do in order for us to survive. My sister's brain infection was long and devastating . . . my family eventually had to go on food stamps. This experience had taught me the value of a savings account, which was fortunate because between 1990 and 1995, we exhausted approximately 50 percent of our personal savings in order to meet our living expenses.

During the up times in the oil market, Carl and I would talk about our "out of touch with reality" flow of money. We had not shared with McKay, friends, or family that work in the oil patch was slow—work in the oil and gas industry is either feast or famine. We were very proud and did not want to admit that we both were struggling with the financial changes that were taking place in our family. Thank goodness we had been prudent savers or we would never have weathered the financial storm. Carl became intense and yet unsure of which direction to go next. The oil patch was slow, building small houses was not profitable, and what we were doing in Amway was costing money, not making money.

Carl worked hard recruiting members, and I worked hard building relationships with them. The meetings were long and draining, and I felt as if blood were being sucked from me. I did not share my feelings of frustration with Carl, which was a mistake on my part. I tried to think and act positively at all times, and because I felt so badly that nothing seemed to be working, I even wrote Carl a letter saying I supported him in his endeavor. I did not share my inner feelings with him concerning our future. In fact, by not sharing my thoughts with Carl, I enabled him to continue with Amway, even though I felt it was not where I needed to be in my life.

68

Chapter Three: 1990–1995

In 1994, I began to feel as I had felt during my pregnancy—as if my safety and security were being threatened. I told myself that I was feeling the old feelings and they were worse than during my pregnancy. In the past, I would have benefited greatly from counseling, but Carl and I were prideful, young, and immature.

I don't remember exactly the incidents or sequence of events that caused me to crater, but one day I felt as if I were carrying the weight of the world, and the burden was unbearable. I called a friend named Wayne—a former member of our Sunday school and a counselor who no longer practices—and I was crying. He asked what was wrong, and I told him I needed help. When I met with him, I remember saying, "You have to help me. Something big is coming, and I won't make it unless I lay down some of the things I have been carrying for years." He said, "Let's get started."

I began the process of healing. I walked through my childhood and the losses I had experienced. I shared with Wayne feelings that had not been adequately grieved because I had stifled my feelings and let fear rule my life. I realized that I was afraid of rejection from my family, but I had grown enough to know that I could no longer keep everyone comfortable while I was quietly falling apart.

I had losses in childhood that I needed to walk through, and I needed to forgive those who had wronged me. I also had unresolved sadness from adulthood. I set out to heal myself by facing those feelings. First, I knew that I had not said goodbye to my old dog, so one day, I walked across the road to where she had been buried near the pump house at Danyana. I had spent almost a year of my life caring for her in old age. At the time, I was working with Carl, and I told him I did not want to put her to sleep until there was no hope, and I wanted to go home and stay with her in her last days. I had to wheelbarrow-walk her when her back legs would give out: I scooped up her hind legs, stooped over, and held them as she moved about with her front legs. She had been my faithful friend through so much, I could not bear to take away any good moments she could have. I cared for her until the end. Eventually, the day came when there was no hope, so Carl drove her to our friend Warren, a veterinarian about forty miles away, and she left this earth. As I sat near her burial place years later, I sobbed and told her of all the things she had done for me.

Another loss I hadn't faced was that of an old friend named Lyle. He was three years younger than me, and we had been friends since childhood. He and his wife moved to Texas one year prior to our move, and he had been killed in an automobile accident. Carl and I helped his wife as she walked through her loss. I had wanted a shirt of Lyle's to wear to remind me of him, and I wore his old flannel shirt of his for years. Wayne once remarked that I was more real in that shirt than at any other time. Now, I knew I had to let go of Lyle, so I took his shirt to the backyard and burned it by my oak leaf hydrangea. I watched as it burned, and I said my goodbyes. That was in the winter. In the spring, the hydrangea bloomed for the first time.

Out of both embarrassment and pride, I did not tell Carl that I was working on my issues. Wayne eventually insisted that Carl know of the work I was doing, so I made the difficult decision to tell him. He was extremely angry at me, which made it difficult to choose to continue my work toward healing. Not until later did I understand his anger, hesitation, and level of confusion surrounding my healing.

Wayne asked me if I felt I was doing better at coping with life. I told him the only thing I did not feel I could cope with would be something happening to McKay.

The next stage of therapy was to work on the rage and anger associated with the losses in my life. I needed to seek the counsel of a therapist who was skilled with intensive rage therapy. Wayne recommended Vernon Van Rooy, whose office was located near Conroe. That spelled convenience, so I was open to the next step: I wanted the anger inside of me resolved. Before I could begin this next step, my life changed.

By this time, McKay was beginning junior high. During the summer of 1995, he talked of going to military school instead of junior high in Conroe.

I did some research on military schools, but we drove by the junior high and he decided that he wanted to remain in Conroe. I regret that drive.

Since McKay and I had a rapport that allowed us to discuss the real issues in life, I shared with McKay my desire to return to work. I felt that Carl was struggling with where to spend his energies, and I decided that it would be in the best interest of the family and me if I returned to the workplace. I wanted to bring some stability to our home, and I assured McKay that we would talk about what he was to do after school and how it would affect our home.

I secured teaching applications from the local public school and the local college. McKay asked me if I thought Carl was going to die and if that was why I wanted to work. I told him I wanted to regain some independence. Then he asked, in a blunt and matter-of-fact way, if we had life insurance. I told him yes, but that was not the point. I wanted to use my talents as a teacher, and since he was getting older and the school did not need a full-time volunteer mom, now was a good time.

Each year before school started, we would spend a day in Spring, a small town nearby. We spent our usual day at Old Town Spring, where we shopped and Carl joined us for lunch. There is a little shop that sells pottery made by the handicapped. I purchased a cross from the shop, and when I arrived home, I got my stepladder and hung the cross above the back door. As I was hammering the nail into the wall, I thought of the captives in Egypt and the hardened Pharaoh. I thought of the blood on the doorpost during Passover, and I prayed. I still grow weak when I recall the prayer—I asked God if He would allow this hanging of the cross to be like the blood of the lamb. I asked Him to keep our home safe.

I went through a period of time one summer during which I focused on a scripture that I read so much I memorized it: Isaiah 45:1–7. One night, I asked Carl to follow along to check my memory. After reciting what I remembered, he looked at me and said I had memorized morbid scriptures because of the reference to God allowing both good and bad in our lives. I told him I needed to plant the words in my heart.

After the first few days of junior high were over, parents were invited to tour the new building and visit with the teachers. McKay walked up and down the hall, not with his best friend, not with his friends, but with me . . . with his arm around my neck. He was excited about growing up and moving on, but he allowed me a place of merit in his life even in junior high.

I drove McKay to school some mornings, and Carl drove him on mornings when he had football practice. One morning during the drive, McKay was full of questions. I thought it was strange that he was not asking questions about school. Instead, he was asking questions like, "When is the end? What will it be like?" I told him I could not answer those questions because I did not know exactly what to expect. McKay said he wanted to know, and I suggested one sure place to find out—the book of Revelation. I suggested we begin reading Revelation, and maybe that would give the both of us a better understanding of the end of time.

That night, we began reading Revelation. McKay was propped up in his bed, and Carl was reclined at the foot of the bed. I chuckle as I remember Carl's surprise when I told him McKay wanted to know about the end of time. Carl said he wished we would just pray, and that we'd not delve into Revelation. I remember his hesitation at reading from perhaps the most misunderstood book in the Bible.

Most of my life I have been a random person. I randomly organize, pack, and clean, but with the Bible, I begin at the beginning, so we began reading at chapter one. When I read the third verse— "Blessed is he who reads and those who hear the words of the prophecy, and heed the things which are written in it, for the time is near"—McKay's eyes were big, bright, and alive, and when he heard the words, he widened his eyes in surprise and amazement and said, "I am blessed!"

I looked at him and realized that I had worked with folks in Sunday school for years, but I'd never seen an adult or a child at this point of spiritual awe. When we finished reading and we had said prayers and good night, Carl and I returned downstairs. I turned to Carl, held him by his arms, and said, "Don't miss this! In all my life, I've never seen a child reach this point. " I do not to this day understand why I was allowed that moment in time with McKay, but it is a great treasure to my soul.

One day after school, I had to attend a Parent/Teacher Organization meeting. I had told McKay where I would be in the building, but he had forgotten. When I was leaving the building, he ran to my side, frantic. He told me he had been hunting for me everywhere. He had even looked in my car to see if I had fallen asleep. The school security guard had been watching McKay and several other children, and McKay was frustrated that he had not been allowed to go back inside the building and look for me. He showed me a tiny drop of blood on his heel, which he had hurt while looking for me. I told him I was so sorry he had hurt his heel and that he had forgotten where the meeting would be held. My heart was racing, and my mind was in high speed with thoughts as to where I had heard the words bruised or hurt heel. Then I remembered: In Bible study, I had been taught the story of Jesus and his bruised heel caused by our inflicting pain on him.

I had feelings of uneasiness and foreboding about life. I understood that my gut was sounding its alarm, but I could not make heads or tails of why. I just knew that something inside of me said there is danger near Carl, McKay, and me.

One day, Carl asked me to give a cosmetics party in the home of an Amway member. I invited other members and friends to the party, and those members included Connie Crawford. When I called to invite Connie to the makeup party, Hilton had answered the phone. I knew he gambled locally over the phone lines, and I had mixed emotions about this, so I said I hoped I wasn't interrupting his important conversations. He did not laugh, and he very seriously said, "I don't do that anymore; it is bad for my health." When I hung up the receiver, I told Carl that Hilton was in trouble with his gambling—he had even used a line from an old movie—and that we needed to stay away from the Crawfords.

We attended the party, and I could not put my finger on the exact moment when I felt Connie was uncomfortable with her surroundings, but when I arrived home, I told Carl I did not want to spend my time with her. I felt that something was wrong, and I found it highly unusual for any female who attended a makeup party where very affordable makeup was sold to walk away empty-handed.

A few days after the makeup party, McKay and I had to drive to the neighborhood where Connie and Hilton Crawford lived. When I stopped the car in front of their home, there was an uncomfortable feeling in the air. I knew in my heart that something was amiss, but I could not make any sense of the feelings in my gut. I remember those moments that I spent in front of their home with a haunting, spirit-like eeriness. I was aware of something, but I couldn't pin down what I was feeling. I have spent many moments beating myself up for not questioning Connie and Hilton, for not asking if they needed help, for asking if they wanted to talk about their comments and behaviors that reflected troubled people. If I had been responsible, I would have posed these questions. Why did I not lovingly confront them? Fear?

One morning soon after, when McKay was coming down the stairs, he told me he'd had a very bad dream. I asked if he wanted to tell me about it, and he said he'd dreamt that he and his friend were in a field. His friend was plowing, and McKay was moving rocks from the field. He said that when he picked up a large rock, there was a snake under it, and the snake bit him.

This was disturbing to him and to me. I remembered the teachings from my childhood: one would be taken, and the other would be left to plow the fields. I went to Carl and told him that McKay needed to share his dream because he was uncomfortable. As we ate breakfast, McKay shared his dream in detail. (I have such mixed emotions when I relay the details of the last days of McKay's life . . . I did not know they were his last moments.) I have thought of the history of my family and the influence of Christianity, as well as the subtle and sometimes joking influence of superstition and voodoo in the South. McKay had heard the same comments that I had heard as a child. He could see the concern on my face as well as on Carl's, so he threw his arms up in the air and said, "But look at me. I'm okay! I'm here today!"

I recall this as one of the most intimate moments we shared as a family. McKay wasn't ridiculed for his dream; instead we listened and we gave support and love. The sharing of one's dreams, thoughts, aspirations, fears, and longings brings a level of intimacy that increases the closeness of people.

During the week before September 12, 1995, Carl and I attended a meeting. McKay did not want a sitter, so we agreed to call several times while we were gone. My gut had a sick feeling about leaving McKay home alone, so that night I left my car parked in the driveway. My stomach was in knots, and I called home so many times he told me to stop calling and that he was all right. I did not know at that time that our neighbors were receiving hang-up phone calls. I feel that if my car had not been in the driveway, McKay would possibly have been taken on this night.

Hilton Crawford had called this week and the week before to determine if I would be attending the Amway meeting. I told him yes. I realize now that it is best that most people do not know a family's comings and goings. I feel that people can have feelings of uneasiness, foreboding, and downright unexplainable fear. There can also be the fear of confrontation. I look back and as they say, hindsight is 20/20. I wish I had dug a little deeper into why I was feeling the unexplainable dread. I wish I had been more confrontational, not in a negative sense of the word, but in a probing way. I wish I had asked more questions of the people I thought I knew. Carl and I had placed ourselves in circumstances where there were so many people, we could not possibly know them all. This was what we thought was the Christ-like thing to do. Now I look at life through a different light. I guard my heart.

Mr. Webb grew sunflowers.
McKay helped Mr. Webb plant a row of sunflowers in his garden.
They grew, they bloomed, and they died.
Thank you, Mr. Webb.
—Paulette

Chapter Four
Tuesday, September 12, 1995

M onday, September 11, 1995, was a typical morning, except for the fact that McKay was very excited about playing in his first football game. As Carl and McKay were leaving that morning, Carl asked him to stop on the back steps to get a picture of him on the big day. McKay had not been interested in playing sports until seventh grade, but his friends and the coaches were patient with him because he did not know all the rules of the game. McKay stood on the porch, wearing his trusty backpack and a big smile full of dental braces and tiny rubber bands.

After school, we ate yogurt, completed homework, and prepared for McKay's first football game. We had dinner with my mother, who was in Conroe helping my brother and his family with a new grandbaby. The ballgame was uneventful. When McKay went to the huddle, we found out later from his friends that the play was called, and McKay's response was "HUH?" meaning "What do I do?" He was allowed to play fewer than twenty seconds, but he played. My mother flew back to Mississippi, and we arose the next day to our routine.

The next day, September 12, Carl drove McKay to school. Normally, McKay did not want us to kiss or hug him in public, but that morning was different for Carl. McKay openly displayed affection toward him. After a period of time, Carl shared with me that something was so different that day. It was like McKay was saying goodbye. I have felt that this was a most special moment of memory for Carl and that possibly it has been a very sustaining emotion for him to replay over in his mind and heart.

I did my afternoon pickup, and McKay was ready for yogurt and homework. I cooked dinner for him, and he ate quickly as he was anxious to begin his assignment. The problem to solve was, *How would you spend one million dollars?* Answering what he'd buy, why he'd buy it, and designing a budget were all part of the problem. He asked me if I would type his answers. I would not do it for every assignment, but on occasion I would type as he dictated. He would laugh when I could keep up with him—I could type as fast as he could talk. It was a game he liked, because McKay was a hunt-and-peck typist who was very slow. He also had to locate some pictures as examples of how he would spend the money. He would dictate a sentence or two, then leave the room, then round the corner again with another sentence or two and a picture ripped from a magazine.

We had an Amway meeting that night, and McKay did not want a sitter. Carl had to go to the meeting early, so he left before me to get to downtown Conroe—about ten to fifteen minutes from home. I left later with our neighbor. When we left, McKay was sitting in a chair in the den eating ice cream from the box. There was a light drizzle, and I told him to keep the phone handy and to call next door if the weather changed. I set out a flashlight just in case he needed it. McKay turned on the alarm system as we left. He had been taught how to arm and disarm the system, and he knew not to open the door for strangers. Once a police officer had come to the door when a neighbor's alarm had been activated, and McKay would not open the door for the police officer.

I walked out the glass-paned, wooden French door. I watched as McKay armed the alarm system. I walked to the car and looked back over my shoulder as a thought ran through my head: "You have done all for this child you can do." It was an odd thought and I have remembered it many times since that night.

When I arrived at the meeting room in the multi-story building, I walked to the large windows of the room in which we were meeting. I don't know how to explain them—I can only relay my thoughts, feelings, and my account of those moments. I looked out the window and had the most lonesome feeling. There was a light drizzle, and as I looked at the street below, a car was driving by. I wondered where a car was going on such a dreary night. My heart was so low, and to this day, I wonder if that was the car McKay was in.

When the meeting was over that evening, some of us met at a local restaurant for coffee around 9:30 or 9:45. As we were leaving, Carl called to get a report from McKay. He told me he did not get an answer, so we thought maybe McKay was talking to a friend. Carl stayed a few moments at the restaurant, and then told me he would go home and stay with McKay. He told me to enjoy my coffee and that his friend would ride home with me.

I ordered something to drink and had just started it when a phone call for Carl's friend came to the restaurant. He left the table, and I paid no notice of him being gone or to his demeanor when he returned to the table. He told me we needed to get home, so I left the table and proceeded to the car.

As we were pulling out of the parking lot, Carl's friend told me McKay was not at home, and Carl could not find him. I began to scream and I crouched down like a wounded animal in the floorboard of the car. When we arrived home, there were people in the front yard. I ran around trying to find Carl. Another of Carl's friends grabbed me by the shoulders and held me as I was screaming, "WHERE IS MY BABY?" In my mind, I can still see the friend's face as he told me no one knew where McKay was—his face spelled fear and horror. My initial thoughts of denial were that McKay had possibly left and gone on a fun ride with a few of his older acquaintances who had recently secured a driver's permit or license.

I quickly brought myself back to reality. McKay was not a perfect child. He was a preteen boy who was full of life, but one thing we knew from past experience—he was not sneaky or defiant. I told myself then that McKay was not with a friend, that someone had taken my baby.

I was told that when Carl had arrived home, a woman with a raspy voice had called the house. My terror intensified as I heard what the woman had said: McKay had been taken and the ransom demand was for $500,000 in $100 bills. McKay would be returned if we did not call the police and if the money was paid. The woman told Carl she would call back the next morning with more instructions. That phone call never came.

The memories and emotions of that night are still alive in me. I experienced total emptiness. There were no songs or dances in my heart, only desolation. Carl came into the house, and I heard him call Connie and Hilton Crawford's house. Carl told me that Connie answered the phone with a question: "What's going on, Carl?" She was not groggy or sleepy- voiced—she went to bed early on school nights. He told her he needed all our friends to help look for McKay, and he asked her to give him either Hilton's motel number or his mobile number. She said she did not know where Hilton was spending the night, and she did not know his mobile phone number.

I was taken to a neighbor's home. My mind was racing. I remember asking someone to call Connie again and ask again for Hilton's whereabouts and his mobile phone number. Her responses were the same as they had been to Carl. She did not know where her husband was, and she did not have his cell phone number.

I began to think about the personal friends I had. I did not feel that any of my female friends would harm McKay. I thought of the male friends I had known for years. I did not want to face the reality that one of them might have taken McKay. I called Wayne's wife and asked her to have Wayne call me since he was in Chicago. He called, and my first question to him was, "Do you have McKay?" He said he did not and wondered aloud why I was asking him that. I told him that McKay had been taken and I needed him to come home.

I went back to my home. The walk across the road was one I will remember for a lifetime. My feet felt as if they were shoved inside two concrete blocks. There was yellow police crime tape greeting me as I walked up the driveway. Fingerprint dust was all through our home. Because of the ransom demand, the FBI had been called. They asked Carl and me to prepare three lists: 1. those whom McKay trusted—those with whom he would have left the house, who had a key, and/or knew of our comings and goings; 2. those who drove a car that fit the description; and 3. all those who were to be at the Amway meeting. When listing the names, I realized that more than likely the person who took McKay would be an individual who was on all three lists. I remember preparing the lists, and as I added each name, I associated that person with trust, love, and respect. I looked at the names and realized that I had to detach from them personally. I knew only one thing: someone had McKay, and I wanted McKay home.

There was one name on all three lists. That name was Hilton Crawford. The man whom McKay referred to as "Uncle Hilty." A man in whose family pool McKay had liked to swim. I lay on the couch in the living room because I could no longer stand on my feet. I felt like a flower whose edges were slowly browning. The moments ticked by slowly. Several people had come to be with me. Somewhere around 2:00 a.m., my body jerked involuntarily, and the impact of the jerk raised me from the couch. In my head, I said, *It is finished; now it will unfold.*

The story of the events of the evening came to me in bits and pieces. Carl was absorbed in helping the police and FBI. I only got maddening snippets of information. I was finally told that when Carl arrived home and found the backdoor ajar, he began yelling for McKay. While walking through the den, he heard the kitchen phone ring. The voice on the other end was that of a female—raspy and soulless—and she demanded a $500,000 ransom for McKay's return. She even requested the money be packaged in a certain manner. She told Carl not to call the authorities, and then she cursed. Carl immediately hung up and dialed 9-1-1. That was when the authorities locally and nationally were notified.

The FBI took charge. Our home was their headquarters. I felt as if our home were the property of the United States Government, something I do not write in bitterness, but out of observation. Carl's office became the location of private meetings, an upstairs bedroom became the polygraph area, and the kitchen was the area for greeting people and keeping food ready and available upon request. The only place where Carl and I could speak in private was in our bathroom.

Phones were tapped as we waited for the return call with details about where to leave the ransom and where to find our precious McKay. Other friends had come to be with us. I was lying on the sofa in the living room when suddenly my left arm began to pull in a palsied manner. Our pastor's wife would straighten my hand and arm and remark that she did not like what they were doing.

Carl was the first person to take a polygraph test. I have to laugh as I remember how the FBI convinced him that the test was highly sensitive and quite accurate. The detectives gave him a demonstration. They hooked him up, asked him if he had ever lied to me, and when he replied no, they showed him that the machine had recorded his untruthfulness. He was convinced, and after that, the test was given without a hitch. I still laugh because I had thought that Carl had never lied to me, and in that moment, I realized my own naiveté. The second person to be tested was Ric, and he was cleared by the polygraph results. This does not mean that once cleared, the individuals who had tested were ignored. Everyone was still a suspect.

The FBI questioned our friend Ric. Ric would help with the dogs, cats, and McKay if Carl and I had to go out of town. The FBI requested that he take a polygraph test, and Ric agreed. They searched Ric's parents' home and all of the outbuildings on their property, which is situated in the country. They did not find any evidence to make Ric a suspect.

I told one of my friends to try to find Smokey at work. He loved his job, and if he were at work, I would know he did not have McKay. I told them to please tell him I needed him to be with me at this time. Smokey and Gail, his wife, and Brenda and Gerald and family came to be with me.

After a designated period of time, the FBI requested that Carl and I go public with the news of McKay's abduction and the ransom demand. I had not known what it was to beg for food or to be in the role of a beggar in any manner. That day, Carl and I were no different from the man on the street corner begging for food. We begged for McKay's safe return.

That week seemed endless. The hands on the clock reflected time moving, but time for me stood still. The little person who had brought life to us and to our home was gone. The house was full of people, yet the combined energy of the masses did not equal that of McKay's. I asked Carl if I could talk with him, so we met in the bathroom. I told him that McKay would not be coming home, and that I was committed to being his wife even without McKay. Carl was not ready to accept my feelings. He felt that McKay could possibly be alive, and he didn't want to give up hope yet; he became frustrated with me. He walked to the bathroom window and remarked that it seemed odd that life would still be going forward without McKay at home. He pointed to the electric meter and said, "Even it keeps turning."

I realize now that McKay had been the dance of our marriage. Our expectations were unrealistic and unhealthy at times, and our desire for material things in life often drove us. We didn't know how to relate to someone of the opposite sex. Carl and I were not open and willing to share all the childhood issues that we had brought to our marriage, and communication of all sorts was stifled. Never before had this lack of sharing of feelings been as obvious as during these first few days after McKay disappeared.

I became a watcher, and I did not do much talking. My body movements and speech became slower and slower. I watched people as they came and went with their words of concern. Sometimes they brought food, sometimes information. I watched the FBI and local law enforcement as they made a tireless effort to return McKay to his rightful place. Law enforcement and volunteers worked until they were exhausted. The FBI left agents in our home during the night. They would work until they found a vacant spot on the floor or a vacant chair where they could sleep for a short period of time. In the early morning hours, the house would be very quiet. Sometimes I would very slowly walk around and look at the people who were asleep on the floor from exhaustion. I felt as if I were in a dream.

I felt adrift in life and could find no reason for the insanity that cruel people can cause. It was a paradox: an individual or individuals were so cruel as to take a child for money, and then those who helped find that child showed concern, love, and dedication beyond hours compensated. It was like looking at good and evil in the same picture. I remembered the words that society would use to describe the acts of kindness—words like dedication and professionalism—but when I heard or saw those who were giving of themselves to search for one little boy, I realized that there are moments in time where words are inadequate to describe the experience.

During this week, time meant everything; yet it lost its meaning without McKay. Each day seemed eons long. My movements were slow and deliberate. The trees, furniture, and people looked as if they had been pushed way back. My visual perception was not accurate: I would think someone was ten feet away, and the person would actually be two to three feet from me. The sounds were of silence at times and at others of a low-flying helicopter. I remember walking out the back door and looking up as a helicopter hovered just above the trees. The entire area around our home was searched.

The silence was deafening. All we needed was one phone call telling us where to leave the money and giving directions on where to find McKay. Neither came, and as the days passed, hope died. I would try to look in Carl's face, and I couldn't. I was crushed that the man who had loved his son so much was totally devastated. Each day became a day of futility and despair, one day dragging on into the next day with less and less hope.

One morning shortly after McKay's abduction, Carl was taking a shower. He was quiet, and I could tell his mind was in full speed, thinking of McKay. He told me he remembered seeing an emblem on the back of Hilton Crawford's car that matched what was described by a neighbor. Carl seemed devastated to again have to consider that Hilton may have taken McKay.

The FBI told Carl and me that they were going to question Hilton Crawford. When they returned, they told us that Hilton did not want to take a polygraph test because of his high blood pressure. I told them that anyone who refused to help a child at a time like this needed to be questioned more.

Carl and I were getting bits and pieces of information from the many friends who came to the house. A service worker at a local car dealership came by to express his concern. We were standing at the bar in the kitchen when he told me that Hilton Crawford had ordered a new mat for his trunk through the dealership where he worked. I told him he needed to tell the FBI what he remembered. He did, and another piece to the puzzle slid into place.

Hilton Crawford was arrested on Friday, September 15, 1995, at 7:00 a.m. at his home in the Rivershire subdivision in Conroe, Texas. FBI agents surrounded his home around 6:00 a.m and blocked his vehicle in so that he could not leave for work. When he came out to get in his car, they handcuffed him and took him back inside. I later learned that he fainted when he was told that they had come to arrest him. He was charged with kidnapping at 1:30 p.m. that same day.

On the Saturday morning of September 16, 1995, Carl came into the bedroom. I was still in my gown, my body was stiff and hurting, and even breathing was difficult. I needed to scream. Carl said, "I want you to go find McKay." I thought he had been through so much that he was having an emotional breakdown. I asked him what he wanted me to do, and he told me to get dressed, go to Connie Crawford, and ask her to help find McKay. He told me to ask Connie and her youngest son, Kevin, to go to the jail and to take paper and pencil with them. He wanted Connie and Kevin to ask Hilton to draw a map to show the location of McKay's body. I felt Carl's fear, desperation, and brokenness. I was puzzled, but I agreed to go.

I told Carl I could not drive myself and that I would need someone to drive. I told him it would be okay for our next-door neighbor to drive me to Connie's sister's home. I got up, got dressed, did my hair and makeup, and put on the peacock pin McKay had given to me as a Christmas present. I needed something to hold onto. Our neighbor's wife drove me to a small lake neighborhood outside of Willis, Texas.

Until then, the time had not come in my life when I felt comfortable praying in public. I did not feel this intimidation as I rode to the house where Carl felt answers could be found. We were silent as she drove. My neighbor respected my silence. She had lost her eighteen-month-old many years earlier, so she knew the hollow void when a child was not present in a parent's life. I bowed my head and lifted my hands toward Heaven and prayed. I knew in my heart that McKay was probably dead, but like Carl, I was holding out hope for the small chance he might still be alive. Someone had to know where my baby had been taken.

When we arrived at Connie's sister's home, I suggested we park about midway down the driveway. It was unusually long, and I did not know what we were getting ourselves into when we entered their domain. I also asked the neighbor to go to the back door and ask if I could visit with Connie.

She walked up the drive and went into the garage. I was watching and waiting for her to come back, but instead, Connie Crawford ran down the drive screaming at me, "McKay's dead, McKay's dead! I know he is dead! Hilton hired a hit man!" I asked Connie, "How do you know? What do you know?" Her only answer to these questions was silence. She asked me how I could be so calm. I told her I was there to find my son.

She yelled and screamed, "They found the car mats. They found the bloody car mats!" She screamed out "Capo," a name that did not mean anything to me. I later learned that Gary Capo and Hilton had both been officers for the Jefferson County Sheriff's Department in the late '60s. I went inside to sit on the sofa, and I was amazed at the cleanliness of the home at a time like this. My home looked as if a bomb had exploded. This one was extremely clean.

Connie's son even walked in with a burger. I remember thinking, "How can you keep it down?"

Connie and her sister were avid prayers when there was a crisis. Once when Connie thought she had cancer, she and her sister had prayed and said the rosary for hours. I realized that I was looking for rosary beads today. If Connie were truly frightened and worried for McKay, she would surely be using the beads. I saw none.

Connie sat on the sofa beside me. She would scream over and over, "McKay's dead! McKay's dead! I know he's dead! Oh, my God! Oh, my God!"

I asked Connie's sister if I could talk to Connie in private. She allowed us to use the downstairs bedroom. As I sat down, my eyes again scanned the room for the rosary beads. In my head I said, *There are no beads for McKay.* Connie sat down and started talking about Hilton, his financial difficulties, and his gambling. I opened the door and walked back into the family area. I told them I needed pencil and paper. They handed me what I needed. I told my neighbor that she needed to get us some help, so she talked with her husband and Carl. The FBI arrived very quickly and sat outside in the backyard area.

Connie spoke of the shipping business venture where she and Hilton had invested money. She gave me the names of the investors. I wrote down the information and gave it to the FBI. I asked her if the shipping was done by truck, rail, plane, or boat. She told me it was by ship. I asked her what they shipped, and she told me they shipped chickens to foreign countries. She said that customs stopped the ship and the chickens spoiled and then they could not be delivered. I asked her if they salvaged any money from the recent bankruptcy, and she said about $20,000. She said that they had taken that money and invested it in another shipping company. I asked her when she knew that they were in financial trouble. She told me she was aware when Hilton had the bills sent to his office instead of the mailbox outside their home. She told me at that point that she could no longer keep track of what they owed and to whom. She said she had told Hilton not to do anything stupid, that they could just start over and rebuild in life. She kept saying, "I told him not to do anything stupid." There was anger in her voice.

The information she shared was new to me. I had not heard them speak of a shipping investment. I asked Connie if she would go to Hilton, and if she would take Kevin, their youngest son, and paper and pencil. I wanted her to stay at the jail until Hilton drew a map showing where McKay could be found. She screamed, "Why didn't Hilton take that gun out on that road and kill himself!" At that time I did not know what to ask. Now I would ask, "What road? What gun?"

Connie screamed in anger, "Hilton deserves what he gets!"

Connie's sister screamed at Connie, "You're stupid! You never saw through Hilton and the things he's done!" She continued, "I should have known something was up with anyone who changes his telephone number that many times."

I decided it was time for us to leave. I had one question I wanted cleared up. I asked Connie and her sister if Connie was taking any medication. I wanted to know if she had been under the influence of any medication when she gave me the information she had. They both said Connie had no medication. Connie's brother-in-law asked me where Carl was because he wanted Carl to see what this had done to his family. I realized then that these people were selfish and emotionally bankrupt.

I left there with my insides in pieces. I felt as if my skin were holding shattered slivers of glass. When I returned home, I lay down and waited in total exhaustion. I knew that it would be only a matter of time before Hilton led the FBI and other agencies to McKay. Either they would find him or they wouldn't. I could not imagine Hilton drawing a map. It would be to his severest personal detriment to give the whereabouts of McKay, especially if McKay were injured or dead. My back hurt so badly. I could not imagine what I had done to cause it to hurt so badly. I told myself that I was hurting because McKay had been shot. I did not know any details at this time, but I felt as if my body had suffered from some of the trauma. I remarked many times about my back killing me.

Sometime early in the morning on Sunday, September 17, Carl came into our bedroom. He knelt beside the bed, and I looked into his face as he said, "Polly, I am so sorry. I wasn't big enough to bring McKay home." Hilton had drawn the map. McKay's body had been found in Whiskey Bay, a swamp. He had been there for many days, and he had begun to decompose.

The next moment my back arched off the bed. The sound coming from me was one of choking and loss of breath. I do not know how to explain what happened next, but these are the moments that began to shape my life for an extra challenge. In my head I said, There goes my heart. *There go my kidneys.* I was not afraid. I told myself that my brain was a computer and that it was shutting down. The next moment, I was looking down on those who were helping me. They had a wet washcloth, and they were rubbing my throat in a downward motion.

The next thing I saw was a screen with me in the bottom left corner. I could hear the sound of a crowd cheering—it was the sound of a large group at a sports event except it was a roar born of a different kind of excitement. From the right lower corner of the screen, McKay entered on the shoulders of six angels. He was laughing and smiling and looking straight ahead. I yelled at him, "Look at me, please look at me just one more time." He continued to face the crowd. I could see his profile and the big smile on his face. The fabric he was wearing was indescribable and beautiful. The six angels did not focus on me. They also kept their focus on the open air amphitheater-type arena. I recall the next thing I said to myself, my "cognitive human" thinking: *Typical teenager.*

And then came a voice, a voice that interrupted my moments with McKay, a voice that interrupted the total peace I was experiencing. That voice said, "You can't stay." No explanation, no discussion, no choice on my part. I had returned to earth.

When I opened my eyes, the house was solemn and quiet. My home had not been quiet since Tuesday. I was flat on my back in bed and I couldn't move. I tried to talk, but I could not make a sound. *I could see.* My focus was clear enough for me to begin a mental chart of what I could and could not do. My mind raced, as if all I could do was focused in my head. I could think rational thoughts during an irrational time. I could see, hear, breathe, swallow, and blink my eyes, although the two eyelids did not blink simultaneously. My breathing was irregular. I thought that maybe the last week was a bad dream, or maybe I had been in car accident that left me unconscious, and now I was waking up. I thought of all the options that would still leave McKay at home, safe and happy.

I heard a repeated tapping on the lamp shade that was by the bed. I could move my eyes from side to side. I looked to my right, and a silly moth was tapping on the lamp shade. This was my first personal encounter with God after opening my eyes. I told myself in the hollowness of my brain and heart, *Watch for the small things.* God is near. I knew this was a sign from God because He was the only other being who knew of the book I had completed reading a few weeks before McKay's death: Chuck Swindoll's *Flying Closer to the Flame.* Dr. Swindoll wrote of man's hunger and how it can be filled, and he explained it by using the analogy of a moth trying to get closer to the flame. We are like the moth trying to get closer to the light.

I began to talk to myself. I would try to rethink the events of Sunday and the words of truth that were screamed at me. I told myself, *You are in a deep hole, and you are in for the fight of your life.* I would tell my hands to move, but I felt as if some other part of the brain were trying to kick into motion. I knew that I couldn't speak right now, but if I could make a sound, then I knew I could make a word. My thoughts were intelligent thoughts. I was perplexed as to why I could not move my limbs if my thought processes were so keen. I could do mental math, why could I not move? I thought of the people who have found themselves with a keen mind and no mobility and speech. I prayed and asked God to let me move. I asked Him if I had lost everything but my ability to think.

Thus began not only my struggle without McKay—now I also had a physical struggle: I had suffered a stress-induced stroke. I don't know how long I lay motionless, my body was rigid and lifeless, unable to cry. I just moved my eyes and tried to see another human.

I remember people coming and going. I remember the pastor's wife rubbing my back and saying she did not know why she was there but telling me, "I am just supposed to do this." One person began to cook for me, and Wayne fed me as one would feed a small infant. I remember I felt as if I were drooling, and I was. I felt as if my hair was matted; it was. I had my favorite purple roses flannel gown on. I knew I was not physically pretty and that I was broken and no one seemed to know what to do. Wayne would tell me I was beautiful, but I had drooled so much I could feel that my hair was crusted. Carl could not be there for me, and I could not be there for Carl.

Wayne asked me if I wanted something of McKay's to hold. I was brought his worn out Wile E. Coyote. Wile E. had even attended church dinner on Wednesday nights. Everyone did what he or she could. Friends tried to fill and meet Carl's and my needs.

I remember being given some medication to keep me from throwing up. I felt it would have been better to throw up my guts and maybe some of my feelings would have come up too. The medicine was so strong, and historically, I had fought medications, as I did not want to be "out of it." I wanted to be as coherent as I could be during this time. I later discovered that the medication I was given is also given to people who are coming down from the withdrawals of alcohol. I thought this odd because I am not a drinker. I remember feeling that if I ever came out from under the effects of the medicine. I would refuse to take it again. I remember being told that my brother, Greg, vomited in the flower bed after he'd heard about McKay's death. I wanted to throw up, too.

I began to make moaning sounds at some point. I sounded like a record on the slowest speed. It reminded me of when we children would turn our record player on slow, then drag our finger on the record to slow it more, then turn it loose and go to full speed, causing the singer to sound like the chipmunks. My world was so bizarre I wondered if I'd go to the chipmunk speed next.

The first words Wayne helped me formulate were *thank you*. I knew Wayne was aware of the rage and anger inside of me, and thank you was not what I was wanting to say. I wanted to tell the world that I would save them the cost of an investigation and trial if they would help me get up, but only *thank you* came out.

I have looked back many times in retrospect and thought about what the Bible said about giving thanks. Did it really mean to give thanks in all things? I have thought of the other scenarios that could have taken place after McKay's death. With many of them, I would no longer have been able to talk, walk, play my piano, write, or share my feelings. This experience taught me to stop and focus on something positive in all things.

Wayne told me I was beautiful to the point that it made me angry. Anger is a powerful emotion; it can be the motivator of positive as well as negative actions. This was good anger. It caused me to begin to push myself even harder. I struggled to move, and move I did. I was determined I would not have crusted hair, so I moved like a robot to the edge of the bed. There was an intense anger in me at the circumstances of the life that McKay, my family, and friends had been required to suffer. I felt that Hilton Crawford and anyone who had any tiny involvement with him and what he had done should be killed in a most undignified manner.

As soon as I could make my way to my office, I slowly opened the desk drawer and took out paper and pencil. My hands, arms, and fingers were extremely weak. My left arm was pulled into a palsied position, and I dragged my right foot. I wedged a pencil in my right hand—not in a handwriting position, but snug enough for me to try to write. I asked God, "Did you allow this to be taken from me, too?" I was able to write, but only in a crude fashion, but I was thrilled that I could at least do something. I told myself "Everything isn't taken. I can still write."

Carl helped me get bathed. It was well over a day before the thought ran through my mind that I might want to try to go to the bathroom. I washed my hair, and it seemed like a lifetime just getting a bath. I was not interested in getting dressed at that moment, so without thinking, I put on my security blanket gown with the purple roses. I began to move slowly through the home with so many people in it who did not understand that I wanted to be alone with my feelings. A doctor who had given me medication walked up to Carl and me and told him I needed to get a bath. The anger in me ignited, and I told him in my very slow voice that I had taken a bath. I realize now that during a crisis or loss there are those who do not know how to be sensitive or just be quiet. This was just a series of words that were totally inappropriate during this time in my life. I have learned that silence is truly the most precious gift that can be given during a time of suffering or a time of loss.

I do not want to sound as if there were not precious individuals who came to me in a veil of silence and knowing. The first person to visit me was a mom who had lost her son in a horse riding accident. I still return to those moments of another mother whose eyes spoke volumes on the loss of a child. Another kind visitor was my sister, who sat crouched on the floor by my bedside just watching and waiting for me to need her.

Other comforts came from the countless mothers who prayed for McKay as if he were their own child. I learned to take a step back and allow others to feel their feelings toward a little boy they did not even know, by whose death struck them with an emotional bolt that sent them to their knees. I am changed by the outpouring of the mothers who ministered to me. Cards, letters, and donations toward the ransom had begun to arrive during the week. Flowers began to fill our home.

I wanted to play my piano, and one of McKay's friends asked me if I'd try. I wasn't sure I could, but after I was helped to the bench, my hands began to move. In the mornings that followed, I was usually led to the living room sofa, where I perched like a parrot all day. It worked fine until those around me would get bored or felt the need to move, and I would find myself sitting alone in the living room. On one occasion, our new pastor walked in and remarked that he sometimes didn't understand why he had come to Conroe. As best as I could, I asked him if he had ever dealt with any other kidnappings. He told me, "Two." My slow reply was, "Now you know why you're here."

September 17—Sunday

McKay's body was found near the exit off I-10 in Louisiana's Atchafalaya basin called Whiskey Bay. Hilton drew a map. This map and the fact that no other involved parties came forward to testify cost him the death penalty.

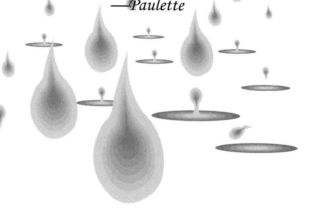

Without you, the slow drizzle of the rain marked time.
—*Paulette*

Chapter Five

Approximately One Year before the Trial

After the news of McKay's death, and due to my deteriorated physical condition, Carl and I were directed to a local psychiatrist. His associate saw us on the first visit. She was a terrific lady who openly shared her hurts and losses in life. I owe special thanks for that one visit of honesty. The psychiatrist had recently experienced a loss in his family, but he was available for our next visit. He was Jewish, and his maternal aunt had died. He cried as he told of his loss. Carl and I needed to cry and to talk, and we were both in shock. I talked, but it was a laboriously slow effort to share my feelings. Carl did not talk much, which was my greatest concern for him. My greatest concern for myself was my mobility and speech impairment. My mind would jump from McKay to the notion that this was all a bad dream and that I would wake up soon. Then my mind would skip to, *How am I ever going to get from point A to point B with the least amount of physical exertion?*

I appreciated the efforts of this psychiatrist. At the time, he served us well. Later on, I found myself evaluating the great effort by the authorities to keep us quiet, but he did help us with many issues that were critical during those first few weeks. He shielded Carl and me from "intense" media coverage, he monitored our irritability and outrage, and he stressed that we be allowed to deal with loss in a dignified and private manner. He also shared his Jewish beliefs.

McKay and I had talked often about what Jesus would hear and see at the Temple, and the psychiatrist told us it is customary in the Jewish religion for family members to prepare the dead for burial. I remembered Carl wanting to go with the FBI when McKay was located. I knew he had held out hope that McKay would be found alive, but I knew from my core that Carl would have cradled McKay regardless of the physical state of his little body. Carl would have lovingly cradled McKay's bones. I felt an indescribable sense of loss that there was no body to prepare for burial.

Our psychiatrist also told us that McKay had died around Rosh Hashanah, the Jewish new year. If memory serves me, he told us that there are more deaths just before the beginning of the new year than at any other time of the year. The Jews go to the synagogue, the Book of Life is opened, and they pray that their family will live through the next year. The decision is made, and the Book of Life is closed. The fates are sealed.

Later, after McKay's burial service was held, I purchased a book about Jewish beliefs. I read it and held on to one belief, a belief of some Jewish mystics. I had a dream shortly after the service, and in the dream, I saw his spirit rise from the graveside, and he was wearing high-top sneakers, shorts, and a T-shirt. He walked away from the grave with long, smooth strides. The mystics believe that the dead spirit walks the earth until the last day of the eleventh month, and then the spirit is released to go to Heaven. I held onto this belief even though it wasn't a Christian belief. In these circumstances, I have discovered that there are moments in time where you hang onto whatever you've got. I think it is termed "survival."

The community tried to help us and themselves heal. A memorial celebration with speakers and music was held on the square in downtown Conroe. A display of McKay's favorite possessions was taken to the local funeral home, and friends, family, and community were allowed to visit what was left of McKay's life.

Chapter Five: Approximately One Year before the Trial

Dr. Avery, a friend, spoke of Joseph of the Bible. As a youngster, Joseph was sold into slavery by his brothers. Later in adult life, some of the family stood in front of Joseph, and they did not recognize him. He told them that what they had done was meant for evil, but the Lord had meant it for good. I took some comfort from this, as I was still trying to find a shred of goodness in people.

There was also a memorial service at First Baptist Church of Conroe. The press wrote that people filed through the receiving line for three hours. I don't remember the time being so long, but my perception of time was shadowed. Time became defined as a series of moments without McKay, times during which Carl and I talked very little. Our focus during this time became how we were to restore dignity and respect to a child who was abused and treated so shamefully.

The altar and front of the church were full of McKay's pictures, toys, clothes, and flowers. There were also samples of his schoolwork and a sign he had painted that said "Goat Cart for Sale" when he was trying to sell his go-cart. The memories were ever present, especially when sunflowers were delivered. They were McKay's favorite flower ever since he had planted them with Mr. Webb. The memorial spoke of a life that was full and alive; it told the story of a person who had reason to go on living.

Before one of the services, Carl took me to my hairdresser after regular hours. Several of the staff wanted to help me by doing my hair and my nails, and since I could not get around very well (it was such an effort just to get to the hairdresser, and I was exhausted by the fifteen-minute ride), they agreed to help me when no one else was in the shop. When I got there, my legs were like rubber. I had not known that the expression "legs like rubber" probably began from some poor soul who had experienced a loss or was scared half to death. I was standing by Carl, and I felt as if I would fall. I felt a hand and arm encircle my waist and support me. I assumed it was Carl, so slowly I turned my head to the right. It seems funny that I would even remember the direction I turned my head, but what I saw made the memory indelible in my mind: Carl's arms were by his side. I thought someone must be behind me, but when I glanced over my shoulder, there was no one. I could only smile; I was entertaining an angel.

The level of exhaustion during these and other events in memory of McKay seemed unbearable, and yet somehow I made it to each dedication or service. I felt as if Carl and I were expected to adjust our grief to a level of public acceptability, or "as society dictates." The agony associated with the death of a child is far beyond words that we have in our language. Society has yet to address some of the issues children face and the agony placed on the child and the parents when a child is abused, abducted, or murdered.

One comfort that helped me through the lonely days and nights was that I didn't have to grieve alone. Of course, I had many alone times, but there were other times when I would think I could not bear to be alone for one more minute, and the doorbell would ring, bringing people there to share the loss of McKay. They would share how crushed they were by the circumstances. They would bring their greatest treasures: their stories.

I felt a closeness to those who shared what time had not erased. One visitor shared the story of his daughter's struggles and how he tried to help her, but how he failed to get the help he needed in order to help her cope. He was an encourager who helped me see the purpose in continuing my therapy. Many people came and shared that they had lost a child. Some visitors were older, some younger, but regardless, they brought their finest gift to me: their stories. Mothers I thought I knew would softly tell that they had lost a child. They had not talked about it in years, but the softness in their voices let me know that it was a mother's love that spoke of the loss. Even though the child was no longer with them, they spoke with a tenderness that made me feel as if the child were somehow still here, if only in their hearts.

Some mothers and fathers detailed losses by miscarriage, some by a stillborn birth. Some lost young children, some adult children. They detailed crib deaths, car accidents, diseases, and suicide, but they all held a common thread of tenderness for their lost child. Once, an elderly man whispered in my ear that his son was one of the first "bubble babies," but there had been no bubble at that time to save his son's life.

As he told me of his son, the same tenderness that surfaced in his voice had been reflected in the voices of the mothers who had shared. I knew then that it didn't matter if one were a mom or a dad, the love was like a deep, underground stream of love that would surface when the child's name was spoken. Losing a child is profound, and I realized that there are some things in life you do not get over—you just move on. There are hurts so deep that words escape the wounded. I learned to ask these moms and dads, "What was your child's name?"

In my journal, I wrote, "The world seems smaller now. It is not such a big place after all. People speak softly in my ear: 'I once had a son.' 'I lost my child.' An elderly woman who stood behind me when I was having my picture taken uttered, 'I lost my son. The load doesn't get any lighter, it just gets easier to carry.' This rang clear when unloading a heavy sack of groceries. I struggled with them until they were manageable. This is how I handled my grief—I juggled and shifted it until I could carry it more easily. I still juggle and shift.

I completed the construction on a home that Carl had begun for clients, and Carl began to work in the oil and gas industry again. It was all I could do to keep up an appearance in front of people while I felt as if I were dying on the inside. I would go to the building location early in the morning and again in the mid-afternoon. I am not sure how the home got completed, other than the fact that I had very caring people surrounding me who were diligent in their work ethic. This period of time, from McKay's death until Hilton Crawford's trial, seemed to pass slowly at times, like I was in a dream.

I did a couple of remodeling jobs, and my workers were on time and ready to work. I had one gentleman who would oversee the work when I could not manage my emotions or when my body was uncooperative. During one of the remodeling jobs, the owner of the company that I used to purchase and install flooring from began sharing his greatest loss in life: his son's death in an automobile accident in which he had been burned. He also recalled returning to the scene of the accident and finding his son's foot, and he shared with me the decision that he and his wife made to have their son's foot cremated.

We had two rituals with the remains. The first was to bury the remains we first received. Then we cremated the remains that were left at LSU (The wound to McKay's head had been in debate. His head was sent to LSU so the forensics could determine if it was a blunt force trauma or a gunshot wound. We did not get the remains from LSU until after the burial. That is why we chose to cremate them.)

Carl and I went to therapy a few more times through the year. The psychiatrist shared his beliefs, and we shared ours, but I felt as if I were drowning. I called Wayne and told him that I needed someone who could help me in a different way because I was not responding to this type of therapy. He gave me the name of Vernon Van Rooy, a therapist who ran a facility in the country near Conroe. I made an appointment and was surprised to find a double-wide trailer as the office and A-frame huts where those who were receiving intensive care lived during their treatment. The facility was state-funded for recovering alcoholics who required on-site treatment. There were mostly men at the facility. Many of them were tattooed heavily. At first, I was taken aback.

I looked around, wondering if I had found the right place. A man approached me who told me I could sit on the porch at the office. He pointed to the double-wide trailer. I thought, this is just great, but I walked up the gravel road to the porch and sat down and wondered what in the world I was doing there.

My eyes were drawn to the roof of the trailer. Across the roofline, peacocks sat perched. I thought about McKay and our love of peacocks. I thought about putting on the peacock pin when I went to see Connie Crawford. I looked up and thought, "Lord, I'm going to take this as a sign and not get in my car and drive off!" I met with the therapist in a small, A-frame hut with a sign above the door that said, "Happy Holler." I walked in to find old, dark shag carpet, the walls lined with carpet, and an old mat on the floor. I said, "All you need is hippy beads!"

I began the journey to healing. I told Vernon that I knew I needed therapy, but "Please," I said, "in the process, educate me." I asked him how I had missed sensing Hilton Crawford's evil. I told him my own internal alarms had been going off, and that I had known something was amiss, but I had ignored it. I begged him to please educate me so that I would be less likely to miss seeing what is important in people.

There was a white marker board on the wall. He took a marker in his hand, and he drew a line down the middle of the board. He said, "This side is for therapy, and the other side is for education." The first question he asked was, "Do you like to shop?" I told him I did. He asked me if I enjoyed shopping at the outlet mall or the larger malls. I told him I just liked to shop. His response was, "Every time you go shopping, there is a Hilton Crawford there who is choosing to act or not to act on that day." He explained that he was not trying to instill fear, rather an awareness so I could shop in a safer environment. The safe environment would come from my heightened knowledge of what might be out there.

After the first trip to this therapist, I called Wayne and asked him what he meant by referring me to therapy with the peacocks and the winos. He told me to shut up and do my work. I was very prideful, and I thought I was too good to be somewhere like that, lying on a brown mat in a room shrouded in shag carpet—carpet that muffled the screams of those suffering emotionally. I thought I was too good a Christian to be told by the therapist that he knew I was a Christian and so was he, but that I had work to do. He had spent the first eleven or twelve years of his life in India, and when he told me he thought he could help me, he warned that he would be asking me to do some things that might seem odd because they were used in Eastern medicine. I told him I'd try them because I was drowning.

Part of the regimen was to take as many hot baths a day as I could. Another part was to have a strenuous workout and a massage several times a week. One day, he asked me if I was uncomfortable doing any of the regimen. I told him I was not and did not find any of it odd. It dawned on me one day as I was shriveling up like a dried prune and that if Jesus were here, he would probably tell me to go wash in the Jordan River. I began to think of my bathtub as the Jordan.

Vernon began to teach me and lead me through my grief in a positive way. I would lay on the mat on the floor and practice deep breathing—taking deep breaths in and exhaling deeply. Then, eventually, saying what I felt as I exhaled. Because I had blocked up my comments and I had been shushed up so much by the authorities, it was not easy to allow the love for McKay or the poisonous anger to pour out of me.

When meeting with the authorities, they would say, "Do this. Don't do that. Wear this. Don't wear that." I felt as if all the personal control of my life were being taken away. I was *shushed* because I physically couldn't talk, and I heard *shush* because they didn't want me to talk . . . until I was ready to explode! So, I was a pretty shushed-up lady who wanted to talk.

As I write this book, I have been watching the Chandra Levy case. This is one of the first times in six years I have been okay with watching TV and the reality of life. I applaud Billy Martin, the attorney for the Levy family. He has directed them in a truly admirable manner. They stood strong in asking for a polygraph test from anyone that might be involved in the disappearance of their child, which is what Carl and I should have done. We should have been more vocal, and this was a mistake on our part.

The therapist and I usually met five days a week in the late afternoon when it was his normal time to go home. There were times we met on Saturday if I was having a more difficult time, and I considered this an unselfish gift to me. This therapy went on for an extended period of time.

Carl was not open to therapy, so one day, when he was next door at his best friend's house, I saw them standing on the driveway. Carl was drinking a glass of tea when I drove to the neighbor's on my way to therapy. I rolled down the window and told Carl I needed him to go with me. I did not say where, so he said okay and hopped in the car. As I was driving down the highway to Happy Holler, I locked the doors, and he asked me where I was taking him. I shared with him my concern that sometimes I could barely drive myself to therapy and that if I needed him, he would not know how to find me. I also did not want to face the same confusion I had faced when I went for help with my childhood issues. I felt Carl needed to meet the person who was trying to help me and who was making a personal sacrifice to do so.

When we arrived, Carl was not happy with the location. I wanted him to be okay, to find a peace with the loss. I told him that the therapist had a fetish for poultry. There was a little duck pond and a large pen for the mourning doves. I was disappointed that Carl did not feel safe in the surroundings of someone who could help him, but I was naive to think that because he grew up on a chicken farm he would appreciate the birds. Carl talked a lot the first trip, and I was relieved that he would open up and share his feelings.

Each trip was an experience that left me more and more humbled. Usually, I arrived a few minutes early just to watch the birds. There were even some chickens, and their aimless pecking around for food taught me that they knew their task and set about it. They did what they had to do to survive—they ate, they drank, they slept, and they went to the bathroom.

While visiting, I would look at the faces of the people who were living on site as they received their treatment for alcoholism. They were broken individuals struggling to survive on planet Earth. I could identify with them in that regard. As I later learned, I could also identify with them in taking one day at a time, sometimes a moment at a time. I was to learn that the rage and anger associated with alcoholism is very similar in intensity to the rage and anger I was feeling about McKay's death. There is a sense of hopelessness and a lack of power over the circumstances, and our acceptance of the circumstances has to find its place.

The therapy slowed me down enough to reteach me to listen to good music. I'd always liked music, but certain music was very calming to me. Some music would stimulate me to feel the deep emotions that were so buried, and all I could do was listen and sob. The therapist slowed me down enough to strike a match and light a candle and watch the flame, watch something that I cannot create. He taught me the value of a long, hot Epsom-salts bath, a walk, a massage, and ten deep breaths when I felt I could go no farther. The panic attacks were severe. The flashbacks were unbearable. The sound of rain at night while riding in a car nearly drove me insane. I would remember the light rain on the night of McKay's abduction, and I'd think of the blood in the trunk lining of Hilton's car. *Was this the sound McKay heard as he tried to escape that dark trunk?*

To drive was a feat in itself. I would work the pedals with my left foot if my right foot was dragging. I would steer with my right hand if my left one was pulling. Many times, I could steer and use the pedals better than I could see because my vision was so blurred with tears. There were times that my body would draw up so tightly that I would look at the road through the bottom of the dashboard and the top of the steering wheel. If my body was not pulling, I was usually beating my steering wheel with my fists. I beat on the steering wheel so much that I broke something, and the wheel could no longer be adjusted to different driving positions.

About six weeks after McKay's body was discovered, his remains were returned from forensics. Carl made the arrangements. We felt very cheated and felt as if friends and family had been denied the opportunity to say good-bye to McKay. Carl visited with the local funeral home and asked if we might have some time with McKay. They gave us those moments. I cannot write of this without sobbing. The room had no flowers, and the blue casket was draped with an Elvis blanket. Carl had sprayed McKay's cologne on the blanket. I could not talk; I could only stroke the coffin and wish that I could hold McKay close. I thought of the rites of burial in ancient rituals and how instinctively Carl did things that day. I watched him move in a realm that I had never seen before. It was a moment of deep respect for the passing of life; I was in awe that Carl just seemed to know what to do.

Chapter Five: Approximately One Year before the Trial

The music was so soft, that I thought at first I was imagining the songs that were playing. They were the same songs I had played for McKay at night. One right after the other was played as I had played. The song that McKay and I liked best was "Surely the Presence." When it began to play, I asked Carl if I was imagining the music. He told me I was not. This was the softest moment for me and yet the most difficult. How could God be so loving to me with the music, and yet not allow McKay to come home? This remains a mystery to me.

Carl asked for a magic marker. He removed the blanket and began to write on the coffin. He wrote what would have been his last words to McKay. I remember writing, "Thank you for gracing my life. I miss the grit fights." I realized that not only were we denied the privilege of having last words with McKay—we were also denied the opportunity to donate his organs. If he had been terminally ill, we would have done both.

There was a moment when the doors to the room were open so that family might enter. My mother ran down the aisle. I did not see her coming. She grabbed me from behind around my neck. She laid her head on my back and sobbed. I thought I would fall from carrying her weight on my back.

At the gravesite I was weak, yet I felt an inner strength. I wanted to hold Carl's index finger, and I reached over to do so, but he would not allow me that privilege. This was the little girl coming out in me. After being told that McKay had died, I only felt safe when I could hold onto an index finger. I was told later that I would squeeze tightly even when I could not speak or move around. Carl was angry with me and with circumstances. The emotions Carl and I had seemed to collide instead of comfort, and I had never been so alone. Our marriage became an abstract relationship, the pieces fitting like a Picasso drawing. I realized again that I did not care what people thought. I raised my hands to Heaven and asked God to please take care of my baby.

We had a request from an FBI agent who wanted to play the bagpipes at the graveside. I agreed with Carl that he be allowed to play, and the agent came dressed in the traditional Scottish kilt. My sister has congestive heart failure, and she has requested bagpipes at her funeral. This, for me, was a gift to my sister. I thought she could hear what she had requested to be played at her funeral.

The agent played "Amazing Grace." He may have played others, but my heart hung on "Amazing Grace" and the echo of the whining notes of the bagpipes. I was deeply touched by his sincere desire to bring his gift of playing that day. The sound was one of feelings, and my emotions were comforted by the song.

As I was waiting for Carl to return to the Suburban, the therapist asked me what my hat signified. I told him that McKay and I would usually find a hat for me when we would go to New Orleans. It was just a fun thing that we did, so I wore the hat we had found on our last trip. It was something that made me smile. The memories of him in New Orleans, having fun, warmed me.

I clung to the memories of McKay in many situations. When we ate in a restaurant and McKay had finished eating, he would hop up and rest on Carl's knee until we had completed our meal. He did this from the time he was able to maneuver until the night before his abduction. This is one of the most special memories I have of Carl and McKay.

Carl remained at the graveside. He stood and sobbed and talked to McKay and apologized for not seeing the evil in Hilton's eyes. I can still recall the heaviness of his sobs and his words of apology to McKay as his large shoulders moved up and down with each sob. It took a big person to apologize at a time like that. I did not know what to do for him, so I tried to respect his space and grief.

After the burial, I paced the floors at night like a wild animal whose baby had been taken. I did not feel human, but I felt more like I was from the wild animal kingdom where one species is food for another. I felt as if I had turned my back to secure food for my cub and he was taken as food. It was not a human feeling I had ever experienced, thought about, or heard about. It is a domain that I visit even years after McKay's death. It is primal.

I realized more and more that Hilton Crawford did not act alone. Irene Flores, a woman who once worked for Hilton, was the raspy voice who made the ransom call. Another friend of Hilton's had hidden the car in a storage unit. And another individual had helped burn the trunk mats from the car. None of these conspirators knew the depth of unselfish love that Carl and I had for McKay. They were and are emotionally bankrupt people. They are a cancer to us all; their displayed depraved indifference has no place in our free society.

I began to look around the house and realize how much stuff we had accumulated that was related to McKay and his life. I had taught school for twelve years before McKay was born, and I had collected children's books during that time. McKay was the beneficiary of all my books, and a greater collection grew after he was born. Reading was an important part of our day, and McKay enjoyed a great variety of books. I thought and prayed about the books and his toys—stuff he called his "worldly possessions." A few weeks before his abduction, he had packed up most of his stuffed animals and placed them in the big attic.

I called the church, and they decided to accept some of the books and stuffed animals. The remainder of the books needed a home. I did not want to have them split up, cataloged, and shelved where I could not visit them. That probably sounds silly, but reading was one of my great links to McKay.

Pennies had become significant to us since McKay's death. We felt as if McKay were trying to communicate with us from Heaven when we would discover a penny in an unusual place. Was McKay placing them for us? Were his angels? On one of my first solo drives after McKay's death, I forgot my sunglasses. I ran back in to get them and upon returning to the car, I found a shiny penny on the armrest in the car. I didn't remember the penny being there before.

Another "penny event" happened when I went on my first outing with lady friends. It was the first trip out of Conroe, and I was to drive myself about twenty-five miles. I forgot my sunglasses again, and when I ran back to get them, a shiny penny was at the middle of the doorway. I bent down and picked it up, then looked around. I don't know what I was looking for, but I knew that pennies were a reminder of McKay. The peace I felt when I found these pennies was unexplainable. I had told Carl of the pennies I had found, and I shared with him that I felt it was a way that God was allowing for me to be comforted. I knew the Bible teachings that once a person is in Heaven there is total happiness and satisfaction and no looking back. Once in Heaven, there is no wish to return to Earth. I did know from the Bible teaching that we entertain angels. But regardless of who was leaving the pennies, they made us feel better when we found one.

Once, Ryan, one of McKay's buddies, called and said, "Miss Paulette, I found four pennies in front of my locker!" When all seemed lost, a penny turned up. I was unable to eat one day, and I could not face the empty chair at the table, so I went to get a burger at a drive-in restaurant. I placed the order and sat staring at the stainless steel tray outside my car window. I glanced away, and when I glanced back at the tray, there were four pennies resting on the tray. They brought me reassurance that I was not alone. Just as there were four pennies for Ryan, there were four now for me. And the pennies helped me know when I was making the right decision.

In 1996, the local community college agreed to visit with Carl and me. While Carl, the college president, and I were standing on the sidewalk, the decision was made to begin a children's section at the college. We glanced down and were face to face with Abraham Lincoln on a copper penny. The initial contribution of books was in the hundreds. In 2000, the McKay Foundation donated over eighty books, and it continues to donate to the library.

The dedications continued. Reaves Intermediate School dedicated their library to McKay on one very touching day. I went by myself to see a plaque with a picture of McKay and special words from *The Secret Garden* presented to the library. The plaque says,

I shall live forever and ever and ever!
I shall find out thousands and thousands of things!
I shall find out about people and creatures and everything that grows.

Sometimes Carl just wouldn't go face another reminder that dramatically expressed the loss of McKay, not only to us but to others. I didn't think I could go alone, but I did. It was a deadly, lonely time in my life. My prayer during the ceremony at Reaves was, "God, if you don't intervene at this moment I feel as if I will have another stroke." My body would often become hard like a rock, and the stress was unbelievable. Peet Junior High dedicated an outdoor theatre, and Geisinger Elementary dedicated a sculpture of McKay with his trusty backpack. Both of these dedications were equally difficult for me; yet moments of loving kindness from the school district, schools, and the children were very healing.

Wayne called months after McKay's death and asked if I had painted. I had not even given thought to picking up a paintbrush, much less producing a painting. I felt so hollow, and to paint meant I would have to feel, to get the feelings out of me and onto a canvas. I told him I did not feel like painting. Before McKay's death and the stroke, I wanted to live to be one hundred because I had so much I wanted to paint. Now that McKay was dead, I didn't want to live to old age. Wayne asked me if I would consider holding a paintbrush. I told him I could hold one, but I wasn't sure my hand would cooperate to paint anything. I went to my art area in the breakfast room, and even though I had a maid at this time, there was a roach or two and a layer of dust on my tubes of paint

I chose a brush, sat in a chair, and just stared at the brush in my hand. My mind seemed like an empty canvas. There was not much there, and I didn't know how to make it work in the arena of my painting. I had coped with my right leg not moving or dragging by hitting my hip with my right fist and saying over and over, "MOVE!" It was as if I had to wait for another part of the brain to hear my voice and process the command of, "Move your leg, dummy." I was so angry at my body for not responding. The norm for my life had been moving quickly. One friend would comment to me when we were shopping or having fun: "You go like a house on fire." I did not know what part of my body I could hit to make my hand paint again.

Wayne called again and again and again that day. "Can you pick up a tube of paint—your favorite color—and just hold it?" I could do that. I don't know how long I sat holding a large tube of the color purple.

"Can you put the brush in some of the paint?" I could do that.

Again he called and asked if I could just smear some paint on one of those things I painted on. He meant a canvas. I could do that. At the end of the day, I was looking at smeared paint, opened tubes, and the painting I had begun before McKay's death. I smiled remembering how McKay would comment about the ones he did not like. There were those he had helped with during the night when he thought I was asleep . . . my precious son and the gift of painting that we shared.

Dr. Gore, a college art teacher, telephoned several weeks later. He wanted to know if I was painting. He did not know of my physical struggles, but he felt that painting again might be therapeutic. I smiled and thought, "One more baby step." We talked a long time about life and about art. He, being an artist and a masterful one, could not help but share his expertise. I received a lesson while on the phone. The first group of paintings I painted were dark and intense. I would paint news photos of suffering because I could relate to the feelings. Eventually, I painted over some of these paintings, but I have kept some as a reminder of that time in my life's journey. Eventually the brush strokes lightened and the colors came to life, but not before I had walked through the darkness.

I began painting again. I would paint and paint and paint. I began painting on wooden boxes that people really seemed to like. I would string beads—lots of beads—to serve as a handle or knob for opening the box. Using beads that were of deep meaning to me was one approach I took to healing myself. I had on earrings that night McKay was taken. On that night, one of them broke, and I had placed it in a Styrofoam cup. I placed the cup in a bottom drawer where I kept my costume jewelry, a drawer my sisters call King Tut's Tomb when they raided it while they were visiting. I used parts of these earrings on the boxes. A return visit to the drawer yielded my grandmother's pearls. I cannot write this without longing for my Mama Lee. Breaking the sewing thread that had held the pearls for years was difficult, but I felt as if I needed to let go and move on.

Months before McKay's abduction, I had traveled to North Texas with Ric to take sculpting classes from an equine sculptor. Lois, my local art teacher, had said I was long overdue in painting a self-portrait. Dr. Gore, one of my mentors, had pressed me to study anatomy. I chose to attempt both with a sculpture of myself. This would be a time to fulfill two requirements of those who were guiding my artsy side. Ric, the teacher, and I talked and laughed, but the work was done in silence or with music. I relate well to music as feelings come from within and leave by way of my hands.

The sculpture was formed while I was wearing clothes. I used horse calipers to measure myself, and then I converted the measurements to the ratio of the sculpture. When I arrived home with the sculpture, McKay had not been happy with me or the artwork. He ran to his room and returned with a handkerchief, which he unfolded and gently placed over the sculpture. It was a moment when our artistic eyes did not see eye to eye.

There was a foundry in Dublin, Texas, called Hoka Hey. I wanted the sculpture in bronze, so we drove to Dublin. I remember thinking the foundry looked to be in the middle of a pasture or field. When we entered, a huge bronze of John Wayne greeted us in the showroom. I asked the owner what the name Hoka Hey meant. He told me that in the Dances with Wolves movie it meant, "It's a good day to die"—to us it means, "It's a good day."

I was asked to fill out a form concerning the work to be done. The form required I name the piece of work. I named it "On the Edge" because the likeness of me is dancing on one foot on a rock with my entire body to one side of the rock. I am balanced on one foot. The owner had asked me what had me on the edge. He asked me if it was my son. I told him no, because I had the most wonderful son. I now call this man the Prophet of Hoka Hey.

My emotions were on a roller coaster during this year. I wrote, "I go to the cemetery often. Why, I don't know. There are a few blades of grass that the caretaker has missed. I touch them as if I am gently brushing McKay's hair. I look at the black granite cross. As I bend down, the sky becomes part of the backdrop to the cross. The blue of the sky reminds me of McKay's eyes. I tell myself to look up and experience the blue of the sky. Today was more than I could handle. I prayed, 'Help me God. Send me some of the grace and dignity you gave to Mother Teresa to mark my steps. My body aches and aches. I am so tired of hurting and trying to explain it away. Please allow me to live in a quiet peace and give You my burdens. They are too heavy for me. I am weary of the load. My cup overfloweth with burdens and hurts. Help me take your yoke and allow You to bear my burdens.'"

The therapist would say, "Tell me how you feel," and I would try to formulate words that would adequately express how I felt, but words would escape me. I felt as if the English language was missing words or phrases for times like this. It was then that I realized silence spoke volumes. I wrote, "I agonize over McKay. I move to the deepest depth of the ocean and speak as the whales. I speak only to God with my groanings. There is no earthly translation."

At this time, I still had all of McKay's pets. Each time I struggled with washing down the dog runs, I would remind myself of the poverty, denial of self, and the menial tasks of Mother Teresa. I watched as each one of the old pets aged, especially Penny, who showed signs of marked aging shortly after McKay's disappearance. The copper colored hair on her snout quickly turned gray. As I learned more and more about caring for aged and dying pets, I was reminded of the elderly people who walk gracefully through the aging process.

Chapter Five: Approximately One Year before the Trial

The quiet moments with Buffy, Penny, Fleetwood, Tigger, Pepper, and Frosty Ho Ho were like the steady tick of the clock. I knew the time was passing and with each moment, they were moving away from me. I would try to stare deeply into their eyes so as not to miss one memorable moment. I would listen to their breathing as they slept, knowing that one day silence would take the place of their breath of life. I knew that the clock was ticking, and once it stopped it could not be rewound with new life for them.

The writings from therapy and the files I kept on Hilton Crawford, his family members, and those who conspired and destroyed evidence grew thicker as I collected my thoughts and feelings and wrote. I became aware that some people are not trustworthy. The moments of clarity not only stung my brain as unfathomable—they also stung my health and my emotions.

I would try to erase in my mind what had happened to McKay by telling myself that McKay was sleeping over with a friend, that he was asleep upstairs, that he was in Mississippi, or that he was with his dad. During the day, I would tell myself that he was at school. Anything, any mind game, not to face the gut-wrenching truth: that my only son had been ripped from this life and no one on that night chose to intervene. All involved chose to be silent—they chose to enable Hilton Crawford to murder McKay.

I kept an extra blanket at the foot of my bed. My body would hurt so badly, and I would have moments of such fear and horror that I would go cold to the touch. I used the blanket to heat up my body, and if I could generate enough warmth, it would sometimes ease the pain. One night I woke up and the extra blanket that rested at my feet was shaped like McKay's body. I was so relieved. The tightness in my body left. I told myself, "The nightmare is over. Don't be afraid anymore. He is home. He is sleeping." I moved carefully so as not to awaken McKay. I only wanted to hold him, but when I touched the blanket, the shape of McKay collapsed. This was the defining moment when I realized that what had happened had not been a dream.

The stroke had left me physically weakened. When I would reach for something, even if it was lightweight, I would have to talk myself into picking it up. Tasks that were once reflex or voluntary became acts of deliberate effort. I had to tell my brain: "Put out your arm, open your palm, rest the plate in your hand, and now roll your thumb over the edge of the plate. Don't drop it!"

McKay's death, coupled with the stroke, left me in a state near hopelessness. I suffered from an inability to sleep and had poor use of my arms, legs, and voice. The stroke caused an intense stiffness in my body; the massage therapists said my body was similar to that of a weakened eighty-year-old. I suffered from intense headaches and severe aching in my joints, and many times certain areas of my skin would feel as if they had been burned. The physical pains in conjunction with the emotional pain weakened my body.

For a period of twelve to eighteen months, I would leave my home around 2:00 a.m. and drive, in a palsied position, to the local Wal-Mart. Two or three times a week I would enter Wal-Mart, secure a shopping cart to use as a sort of "walker" for my stiff and aching body, and drag myself up and down the aisles of the store until I was totally exhausted and my body could move more fluidly. I had to completely wear myself out physically so that I could return home and sleep, the only time I had any peace. In my sleep, my mind slowed, my body calmed, and I sometimes dreamed about McKay. In my dreams, he would speak to me, which made the world of sleep one of life's most precious gifts.

I stayed in our home by myself during the week. The nights were the most difficult. The period of time between 3 and 10 p.m. was horrible. Since McKay had started kindergarten, those hours had been my time with him. We would eat together, and I'd help him with homework, watch him play, watch as he practiced piano, rock him, and read him stories. Now, the most I could hope for during those crucial hours was to get a few hours of sleep. After three or four hours of sleep, I'd often sit straight up in bed with fear, or I would awaken hopeful that I had been having a nightmare.

I was too full of pride to go to physical therapy, so I began golf lessons at Wayne's insistence. I wore McKay's golf glove, which had holes in it. My first lesson at Panorama Country Club took a different route after the pro tried to help me swing a club. All I could do was practice balancing a club on my left index finger and rocking it back and forth. My instructor had realized how weakened my body had become. The thought in my head that day was, "I want to hit the ball!" but I realized that my physical limitations were greater than I had wanted to face. My mind was willing, but my body was slow to respond.

I struggled with the lessons. I began to play golf on Sunday afternoons with Wayne and other residents of Panorama. I would play one hole, make it in twelve to sixteen shots, and be totally exhausted. After four or five weeks, I tried playing three holes of golf. I graduated to six holes of golf months later. It took me about a year to build to nine holes.

The first time I played over nine holes, I sobbed as I stood on the green of the twelfth hole I completed. Most days, I just played "goofy golf," as Wayne calls it. I parred the first hole I played, and I quit. It was fun to be able to say I parred every hole I played.

Reading about grief helped me, so I learned about George Washington and Valley Forge, Abraham Lincoln and all of his defeats, and others who have helped form America. I gained courage by reading about their valiant struggles. I read the Bible with a new realness as well.

One book my therapist recommended that had a profound impact on my life and attitude was Victor Frankl's *Man's Search for Meaning*. He shared his experiences of being a prisoner in a concentration camp, and he openly and honestly relayed details of people who would give up, lay down, and die. I knew I was near that point many moments, and I had to make a conscious choice to get up in the mornings, get a bath, put on my makeup, do my hair, file my fingernails, clip my toenails, get dressed, eat something, pray, read something of value, listen for God's voice, and wait on God to reveal Himself in all of the blood, suffering, heartache, and loss.

My physician recommended I take vitamins, and he stressed the importance of B complex. I'm sure he did not intend for me to take as many as I did, but I took them at intervals during the day until I could feel my body begin to feel stronger.

I suffered unbearable headaches throughout this time. I would walk up and down the street with my right leg dragging and my left arm pulling. I would pray and pray about the headaches. I wanted God to at least take the headaches away. I could not understand why He would not give relief for such a simple thing as a headache.

One morning, I awoke without a headache, and I was so grateful. I even enjoyed my bath and getting dressed. I moved smoothly and slowly so I would not jar my head and cause it to begin hurting all over again. After getting dressed, I decided to spend some time looking at my flowers in the yard. While I was outside, I heard someone at the front door. It was a lady I knew from church; she did not customarily visit so seeing her was unusual. She is a positive lady and not a complainer, and she just dropped by to tell me that she had been praying to God about me, and she asked God to allow her to bear one of my burdens. She said that ever since she had prayed, she had been experiencing the worst headache. I laughed and told her that I was having a wonderful day because I had relief from the horrible headache that had plagued me for months. I had heard the scripture about bearing one another's burdens, but I had not thought of it in this light. This was another spiritual awakening for me.

I visited recently with the lady who bore my headache for an afternoon. We talked about that day, and she and I both remember the lasting impact this has had on our beliefs. She and I laugh because she is not the type of person to even admit that she has a headache. She is still amazed that she drove to my home to share about her prayer and a headache—a shared moment of one believer carrying a burden for another.

My life seemed foreign, and I no longer felt a part of this species. I did not know where to turn at times or what to do to fill the time. I wrote even though my limbs were not cooperative. I pressed Carl to take me to the district attorney's office and the sheriff's office, but he didn't want to take me. I look back and realize that he was probably embarrassed by me, but I finally persuaded him by threatening to call my crazy little aunts. I told him I would get my aunts to take me there and bring me home, and I did not have to say more. Carl, Carl's best friend, his wife, and I went to the district attorney's and sheriff's office to share what had transpired on the Saturday visit to Connie before McKay was found on Sunday.

I shared the pertinent information, and I also shared my feelings that there was no rosary visible for McKay in the home I was in that Saturday. I told the police that I knew Connie's habits, and when she was anxious, worried, or scared, she would say the rosary. The lack of beads told me she had already known McKay's fate. I had looked in the laundry, kitchen, dining room, living room, and downstairs bedroom. I had gone there with a secondary motive in mind. I went looking for rosary beads. It was not until I told law enforcement about the lack of beads that I was told that Connie *had* brought her beads when she spoke to the police. Connie had been wringing some beads while she was questioned, and when she was asked to take a polygraph, she refused and just twisted the beads. Some of the officers later told me that they thought she was trying to appear innocent by using the beads.

I continued to feel frustration and anguish over the fact that the people involved in McKay's abduction and murder had not been brought to justice. There were opportunities to save McKay's life, but no one shared the information that may have given him a chance. On that night, Connie lied about Hilton's whereabouts and her lack of contact information for him. Hilton's former employee had made the ransom call in exchange for money. Hilton's friends burned evidence and hid the car. Many times, authorities said that a few minutes may have made the difference. Oh, how I wished that someone . . . any one of those people . . . had spoken in time.

A representative from the district attorney's office, however, was once blasé enough to say that a few moments would not have saved McKay's life, and I was infuriated. I remember being so weak physically and emotionally that I could not climb across his desk and get to his face, but I did all I could I do. I told him I hoped he remembered his attitude when he was one day in the emergency room and on the brink of death, and the doctors and nurses took the same attitude that he had with McKay's life. When one is dealing with human life in jeopardy, seconds can mean the difference between life and death. I am furious as I write. I still have not forgotten this attitude. Even today, I find this attitude in a public servant—one who is supposed to be seeking justice—to be completely unacceptable.

I tried to go shopping with Carl on Mother's Day, but I was so overwhelmed in the mall that my body shut down, and I couldn't move. I was angry at myself because I couldn't maintain the appearance that everything was all right. People in the mall who recognized us would know something was wrong. It was a living hell to try and shop on a day when I could only think of my baby being hurt, tortured, and shot. I still dwelled on those people in the sidelines who had destroyed evidence and bought Hilton Crawford time by offering no phone numbers, no information, no nothing. I know that if someone had called me and asked for my husband's help finding a child, then if Carl were not there, I would have gone to my knees in horror, and I would have told everything about Carl Everett down to whether he liked his socks tied in knots or folded. I will not enable people to commit nor cover up a murder.

Ever since I had the vision in which I saw McKay being carried into Heaven by six angels, I had fretted over the identity of the angels. I felt as if I should have known them, but I didn't. I could not understand why there were six angels for one little boy. One afternoon, I was visiting with a lady who was being supportive by providing me with an opportunity to help her remodel her home. I shared with her the experience of seeing McKay in Heaven on the shoulders of six angels. She began to weep openly and told me of the prayer she said when she was notified that McKay was missing. She has three children, and she prayed to God and told Him that she wanted the guardian angel of each of her children to go to McKay. Her children began telephoning expressing the feelings that had occurred around that time. One child had to pull off the road and couldn't drive for a while. She told me she knew who three of the angels were.

While playing golf, I talked to Wayne about the three angels the woman had told me about. I told him I was still pondering why there were six. Wayne was standing on one of the higher greens in Panorama, and I can still picture him as he was telling me that he knew who the other three were. My immediate response: "Who?" He told me, "Carl's guardian angel, McKay's guardian angel, and Paulette's guardian angel." I have been at peace with this question and its answer since that day.

Carl and I tried returning to church, but it was too early. After returning home, I spent the afternoon in the fetal position in my dark closet, in unbearable emotional pain, asking how a loving God could allow such cruelty. I had asked Him that in my prayers long before McKay's death. Even long ago while I was attending Mississippi College, I had been uncomfortable sitting in my Old Testament class because I couldn't understand how a God could allow the death and destruction of children.

I again returned to church the Easter after McKay's death. Wayne called and asked if I'd meet his family for worship, and I did. That was the beginning of a return to a God I did not understand. I was mobile, but apparently not mobile enough to wear my standard Sunday attire: nice dress, high heels, matching jewelry. As McKay would say, "My mom is all matched up, and so am I." Wayne's daughter remarked that she did not understand how I could walk in high heels, and I told her it took practice. That morning after services, as I was making my way back to my car, I walked out of my heels and was left standing in the grass. *Practice, just practice*, I told myself.

All my life, I have been sensitive to weather changes. I have been "old" in my right hip for years, and if the weather is going to change to cold or rain, I feel it in that hip. After McKay's death, my sensitivity to weather intensified, but in a different way: now, the sights, sounds, and smells of the weather's changes caused me to flash back to different times during those first few hours and days when McKay was taken. His abduction became my point of time reference, and almost every conversation I had began or ended with a reference to "before McKay died," or "after McKay died." Now, my most devastating, overwhelming moments were when I was in a car at night, and a light mist would be falling. I would have feelings surging through me like an electrical current, and I would have no idea what to do with the intense emotions. If I heard the sound of tires on the road, I would wonder again if it were the sound McKay heard on that terrible ride to Louisiana in the trunk of Hilton's car. Or the reverse—on beautiful days, I was reminded that McKay had been denied the opportunity to experience any more of these times on Earth.

This year before the trial was the most difficult of my life. My rage and anger had reached an unexplainable level, and the district attorney's office was still giving only bits and pieces of information to me. Carl went almost every day to their office, and I became uncomfortable with the relationship he was developing with the attorneys who were to represent McKay. I felt that if Carl and the attorneys became friends, it would be difficult to hold them accountable if need be. There was a male attorney and a female attorney who represented McKay, and I wanted them to do their best and to prosecute all who had been involved in McKay's death.

Sometimes, our rage would become so intense that Carl and I would find ourselves thinking terrible thoughts about Hilton's two sons. We were extremely disappointed in their behavior after their father's arrest. They had removed items from their parents' home, and to this day, no one knows if they removed any evidence. There is a side of me that wanted to harm them because I wanted Hilton and Connie to know the pain I had experienced.

Instead of bodily harm, I tried to hurt something else they had loved. Connie and Hilton had two sago palms in the front yard of their home, and the trees were their pride and joy. In my mind, I named the two sago palms Kevin and Chris, for their two sons. I purchased rock salt, Round Up, and diesel fuel, and then Carl would drive me to their house, and I would pour. Those plants did not die, but they got mighty sick. During the winter after McKay's death, Connie put covers on the palms to protect them from freezing. If I were her, and my husband had killed someone, I couldn't have cared if everything in my yard died. I was so offended by her gentle care of these plants and her refusal of information on the night McKay was taken that I even crawled under the covers and poured more poison on the palms . . . all to no avail. One evening, Carl was so distraught that I became concerned at what he might do. I went to the refrigerator, pulled out a dozen eggs, and told him to get in the car. He did and we went to Rivershire. I drove around the block while he egged her house. I figured egging her house was better than harming her or her children. The only problem we had that night was that I cannot see too well in the dark, and I drove past Carl twice before I saw him; he was furious.

There were other times that I knew Carl had been up to some teenage mischief, but I did not ask too many questions. There were times I myself wanted to kill or to hurt their family as much as they had hurt our family.

During this time, I wrote in my journal: "I speak the language of loss. The vocabulary is new to me. The language is laced with words that I have heard, but I can not relate. The words have no meaning or depth of understanding. The language is simply deep moans and groans. The language is broken into sounds that evoke emotion. Now that I know the language, can I become a translator for others? Having been through this experience, I can tell you of the countryside and the stops along the way that are to be your journey. The land looks the same as the land everyone else sees, but after you have endured a loss, everything changes subtly. Even though the food looks the same in this new land, the morning eggs at breakfast will taste different. Food, drink, and touch all will come into clearer focus. Personalities of people will be clarified. You will listen carefully to the words spoken by all, and you will discern insincerity a mile away. Sounds are clearer and more distinct. A freedom will come for you to be the individual you were born to be. There is a mountain to climb in this land. It is the mountain of resting in the love that was known, not in the memories. The memory fades, and you will not remember everything of your visit nor of your days before the loss, but you can rest in the love of the journey."

I often longed for the memories of McKay to resurface; I wanted to look out the window and see him in Carl's favorite holly tree, clinging near the top and hanging on like a cat that didn't have the courage or know-how to back down the trunk. I remembered how Carl noticed the swaying and rescued McKay. He didn't yell—he only wanted him safe with two feet on the ground.

Our marriage became a specimen placed on a slide, held under a microscope, and scrutinized. The shallowness of Carl's and my relationship had caused chaos. Why hadn't I noticed it before? Why did I notice it now, at a time when I needed to feel surrounded by those who would possibly understand some of my feelings?

Carl wanted to go visit the cemetery during the day, but usually someone would stop by and talk in the daylight hours. I wanted time alone with my loss of McKay, so my trips to the cemetery were late at night. Carl would drive me to the cemetery if he were home. If he wasn't, I would drive myself. I wanted to lie on the dirt and try to give McKay a hug. Time after time, I would pray and sob.

I held onto the belief of the Jewish mystics, and at midnight on the last day of the eleventh month, Carl and I went to the cemetery. He stood to the side and allowed me time alone as I slowly made my way to the graveside. I raised my hands to Heaven and prayed and talked to McKay. I told him I now understood he was to be freed to do the work of Heaven. I told him I knew he was no longer earthly bound, but Heaven sent. I told him I wanted him to be free to be all he could be in Heaven.

As I said these things, I cried. My eyes watered and my nose ran. Once a prim, proper, well-educated, multi-talented woman, I was now a broken lady who stood with head bowed, hands raised to Heaven, and mucous dripping to the ground in surrender to life's circumstances. I was humbled. And I share with you now one of my most private moments of grief.

As the trial grew near, I was told many things: wear this and do not wear that... until I was totally disgusted. I just wanted to be me. I am artsy at times, maybe present myself as sophisticated, but I was disgusted with the power and control issues of the district attorney's office. I decided to allow my hair to be natural. I have colored my hair since high school, when my natural color was mousy brown. When my brother died in the car accident, I went gray on top. With McKay's death and my getting older, I was past salt and pepper—I was 95 percent gray. With all the frustrations with the trial, I decided to allow the hair color to wear off and become gray. I felt gray. I felt old and used up. Carl became frustrated with me and my decision. He was accustomed to my looking put together, matched, and younger looking than I really was. Even McKay would not have been happy with my decision. When we has alive, he sometimes told me, "Mom, you've got it, you've really got it." Sometimes we have to make decisions that frustrate others, but our decisions are a means of expressing ourselves. I considered Carl's frustration with my appearance and realized that over the years he had worn me on his arm. Now where would he stand with a wife he could not wear on his arm?

With jury selection and the trial growing near, I was faced daily with the realization that I would finally get some of the questions in my mind and heart answered ... I hoped. It seemed we would forever hit obstacles during this course of justice.

Carl and I received notice from the district attorney's office that they did not have enough blood material to do DNA testing on the evidence. In order to get a DNA match to the blood stains on Hilton Crawford's clothes, Carl and I had to give blood. Hilton would not admit that the blood splatters on his clothing were from McKay, so Carl and I were sent to the lab at the sheriff's department. At that time, Carl had a phobia of needles, so when the lab technician asked that we make ourselves comfortable at a tall, bar-like area, we sat on the tall stools and discussed who would be first. Carl decided that he would give his blood first. I told the technicians that Carl had a history of fainting when a needle came his way. As soon as the needle touched his arm, the stool on which he was sitting began to tilt backwards, and his head began a slow motion fall toward the counter. I knew I could catch his face before it hit the counter, but I wouldn't be able to catch the rest of his body, so I yelled for help. The technician could not see Carl's face, so he didn't see how pale Carl had become—even more pale than the typical ashen gray color he had become since McKay's death. The technician came to the rescue, Carl regained his composure, and the blood was drawn. We all helped him to a comfortable seat in the waiting room while I gave my sample. I will admit that I had my moments of wondering, *What next? What else will Carl and I be asked to do? When is enough, enough? What if the blood doesn't match? Then whose blood could be on the shirt?* Two of Hilton's friends had destroyed evidence by burning the car mats from the trunk of Hilton's car because blood stains were on them. Another friend owned storage sheds and had hidden evidence there. Hilton had delivered his shirt to the laundry after he returned to Conroe. The technicians recovered the shirt and sent it, with the samples of our blood, for testing. We were told it would take some time to get the DNA results from the lab.

Patience, I told myself again and again. Circumstances come and go. The therapist once mentioned the word "transcendence" and reminded me that there are people who can walk through hot coals without getting burned. I was reading one book during this time that said something about losing your mind and coming to your senses. I felt as if I had lost mine, but I wasn't sure what was meant by coming to your senses. The most common line I heard from my therapist was, "Things are as they should be."

We began to review the court proceedings so we'd know what to expect. The district attorney's office wanted Carl and me to be prepared for what could be possible questions from their office as well as from Hilton Crawford's attorney. I was not overly concerned about court. Going or not going through the court system wouldn't bring McKay back. I continued to push the district attorney's office to pressure Connie Crawford for a polygraph test, but they would just tell Carl and me to keep the focus on Hilton. They felt she would plead spousal privilege or the Fifth if they tried to test her about any involvement in the murder.

I tried to do as the therapist requested, which was to take care of myself. I had prayed after McKay's death that God would send me what I needed since I could not do for myself at times; I could not meet my own needs. I liked to read, so I began reading about grief. The first book I read was a psychology textbook of Wayne's: the studies of Elisabeth Kuebler-Ross. She studied the stages of grief by working with the terminally ill, and she found that they grieve their own deaths.

I am not sure I agree with all of her studies, but her book helped me realize that grief comes in stages, which I began to call waves. The stages she describes are (in this order) denial, anger, bargaining, depression, and acceptance. I did not seem to go through the stages sequentially, but often randomly and sometimes all five of them in one day. After reading her work, I thought that when I got over being angry, I was finished. I didn't have a clue about the length of time it takes to accept that a loved one has died.

I pinged around in the stages like a mad woman. When Hilton Crawford made the decision to abduct and murder McKay, and when his friends and family covered up his actions, they threw McKay's life into a river of insanity. That river of insanity flowed through my life and drenched the banks of my soul and heart with horror. In a single day I could experience depression, then denial, then anger. Acceptance wasn't part of my vocabulary yet.

Once, when I was in desperate need of something new to read, someone mailed me a packet of Xeroxed pages that contained comforting passages from books, articles, etc. I don't know who sent it, but the package was such a blessing. I considered it an answer to my prayer to God to send me what I need. I have kept the package as a reminder of God's infinite power to meet my needs.

Another day, I received *My Dream of Heaven*, by Rebecca Ruter Springer. The book was written by a lady after she had suffered an illness that kept her near death for days. As I was reading one evening, I came to a paragraph where she described what she referred to as a place called Heaven. She spoke of the clothes the people wore and of the beautiful fabric from which the clothes were made. I bolted upright in the bed and told Carl, "She saw what I saw. It was the fabric that McKay wore as the six angels carried him."

The stacks of books grew and so did my awareness that I was not alone in grief. The knowledge did not lessen my pain, but I no longer felt as alone.

The district attorney's office finally called with a definite date as to when jury selection would begin. They told me they thought I would be the first witness. They asked that I give some thought to how I would dress during the trial and also as to how I would deal with stress of the day-to-day process. I had one dress that was very comfortable, but it was tattered and torn. A lady named Melba asked if she could to something for me, and I asked her if she could repair the dress to a point where it was presentable.

She worked and worked on the dress and the results were beautiful. I was touched. Melba later died of a huge cancerous growth in her abdomen. While she was ill, she continued to work, sing in the choir, and help others. Her attitude was beyond amazing; all of us could take a lesson or two from Melba. I was inspired, so I wrote about her:

Worn out lace and nimble fingers

The occasion was not one of bearing.
The dress was old and long past wearing.
The dress was country, I was told.
It was old.
The dress was a reminder of me.
I just wanted to be.
It was frayed and seemingly beyond repair.
She had just come to share.
Was there anything she could do?

Could she bring comfort to these ruins too?
The dress had frays that numbered as the sands.
I asked if she could sew with her hands.
With needle and thread she lovingly sewed.
To the worn out lace a gift she bestowed.
The nimble fingers brought insight.
Humankind again had bright light.
That moment was a simple gift.
That caused my heart to lift.
Of many gifts I have read.
Of this I have said.
There was none to compare.
To a gift laid bare.
Of worn out lace and nimble fingers.

There is life even at the deepest darkest level of the ocean.
—Vernon Van Rooy

Chapter Six
The Trial

I never gave much thought at the time to writing about the trial and what I saw, thought, or felt. From the beginning, I felt the trial was only a societal formality, and I did not expect much to be gained for me in the way of satisfaction or healing.

I was unfamiliar with the judicial system, but while cleaning out McKay's things, I came upon some of his work from seventh grade. His class had been studying the judicial system, and he had taken notes. It was uncanny that as I was trying to get a general overview, McKay's own words helped fill me in as to what to expect. It was like a piece of the puzzle and a way that McKay could still be a part of what was happening. It was comforting to me. Again, another mind game to help me survive the stress of a trial.

Reading his notes, I found that there were five stages that we had to walk through:

1. Pretrial hearings
2. Jury selection
3. Trial
4. Sentencing
5. Possible execution

I made up my mind that I could walk through these five stages, and they were a piece of cake compared to where I had tread.

I was thrilled to learn that at some point Hilton Crawford would be moved from the Montgomery County Jail to Walker County. With Hilton's being so near, Carl and I had often sat outside the jail at night, just watching the exterior walls and wondering what part of the jail Hilton was in. We would talk and wonder if he could feel us outside the walls.

At one point, Carl had followed a law enforcement car carrying Hilton Crawford in the backseat. Carl had phoned me saying he had Hilton in his sights and that all he had to do was pull the trigger. I told him to go ahead and kill him. I also told him that as crazy as the world is today, he would be charged with murder and that the world would probably delight in placing him in the same cell Hilton had been in. I told him he had a decision to make, but he needed to weigh the consequences of being put in the same cell Hilton had been in. Needless to say, he watched the deputies unload Hilton at the jail and take him back to his cell. Hilton knew Carl was there, I am sure that Carl delighted in making Hilton uncomfortable. I would have.

I wondered how Hilton felt being on public display. I knew that all of us have things we have done that we are not proud of, but we certainly would not want them on the front page of the *Conroe Courier* or on the evening news. I hoped Hilton would die of embarrassment as the truth unfolded, and it would save the community the expense of the trial. It was evident that he did not know that the truth unfolds, and we are left to face our issues when it does. It is my belief that when God set the Earth on its axis, He also set into motion a series of laws we sometimes overlook. I believe that our wrongs will be exposed.

During the pretrial hearings, they discussed the fact that Hilton was indigent and in need of legal counsel. They also debated whether too much press coverage had biased the community. I heard the words until I was ready to throw up. I thought, *What has this got to do with anything?* I just wanted to get the process started so it could be over with. The change of venue was discussed, argued, and hashed out . . . and eventually the trial was moved to Huntsville, Texas.

Hilton went through a string of attorneys before he got his final appointments. An elderly man named Adams who'd prepared Hilton's taxes and helped with the bankruptcy was the first that was called, but he didn't work out. Another attorney, Wendy Akin, wanted to take the case pro bono, but we were told that Hilton's wife didn't feel she was the best. Mike Ramsey was then retained with Cynthia McMurry, who would do the trial work. We were told Mr. Ramsey promised future legal assistance for Hilton's family and others who might potentially be charged.

McMurry came from Houston. I can't think of a better word to describe her than odd. She was a blond who wore her hair shoulder length, and when it got in the way, she would grab a "scrunchy" from her briefcase, and within a few seconds, she would be wearing a ponytail. I considered that very disrespectful in a court of law. The rumor in the small town of Conroe was that she was dating Frank Sinatra's son; nevertheless, she didn't last long, and Rick Stover and Lynn Martin were finally appointed by the court for Hilton.

I attended some of the pretrial hearings, but not all. I became bored and put out with the call for justice for *Hilton*. Somehow it did not make sense to me that there were those calling for justice for Hilton. Even though I did not know every detail from the district attorney's office, I did know that Hilton Crawford would not have been arrested and charged with capital murder if there had not been sufficient evidence.

Judge John Martin set bond at $1 million because Hilton told another inmate he would lay low—"leave"—when he got out of jail. The bond was later reduced to $450,000—still more than anyone was willing to pay to have him in the streets.

I was shocked by the number of good people who did not believe in following the letter of the law where capital punishment is concerned. I feel there can be no shades of gray in justice. It was a point of concern for me when I would watch television and see anti-death-penalty protestors, most of whom were from another country, protesting in America—and Americans were listening and doing what they asked! I later learned that some death row inmates receive financial support from wealthy females from Europe. Communicating with and supporting American men on death row seems to be a pastime for some ladies of wealth. I would like to introduce these ladies to a greater cause: educating the children of this earth on how to be safe.

Why do children need to be protected? I strongly feel that there is an element in society that is a parasite . . . a cancer . . . an author of chaos. This part of society must be treated aggressively, or our country and our lives will be in chaos. We cannot fathom the depths of evil in some humans. For good, moral, law-abiding people to believe that evil like that exists is unthinkable and abhorrent. We have a place for those who cannot live in peace and harmony with society, and we know these people exist. It would probably behoove us all to take a stroll down death row. If you question the existence of evil, a short visit might clear your head, or perhaps you may want to view the photos from a crime scene where an innocent child has been murdered or a loving friend killed.

It was tough for me to realize that even good, Christian people can have skewed, depraved thinking. We like to believe that there is good in all of us, and we certainly don't like to believe that any female could be a party to harming a child, or that any mother could murder her own young. Yet, the media proclaims both: someone called a "friend" can and will abduct and murder a child. Mothers can and do murder their own children. If punishment is to be a deterrent to crime, I felt and still feel today that it is time to give the stiffest punishment possible. We forget the first three chapters of Genesis: Cain murdered his brother, Abel. Evil has been around for many years, and it's time to stop it. Vernon, the local therapist, would say something similar to what is in Genesis when I would worry about the truth being delivered at the trial. He would reassure me by saying, "Dead bones speak." I would talk with McKay and tell him we were listening for him to speak. His blood gave us answers.

♦ That smile! Even at an early age, McKay showed emotion when playing the piano. He expressed his emotion by what he played and how he played it. I miss the music he brought to my life.

This photo was a Christmas gift for McKay's father. It really captures the bond between McKay and me. He was my greatest prize. ♦

◆ McKay loved to wear wristwatches and penny loafers. It always made me worry he was growing up too fast.

◆

The children in our neighborhood all had their faces painted to enhance their Halloween costumes. McKay roared and huffed like a dragon in this costume.

◆ McKay had a desire to dress up, memorize lines from movies, and perform. This desire was intensified by his dressing as film characters for Halloween. It took many cans of yellow spray paint to cover the felt hat McKay wore with his film-character costume on this particular Halloween.

He had no lines to memorize, but McKay had a lot of sword-fighting practice to do to prepare for his role as the Mouse King in *The Nutcracker.* McKay was so proud of that performance.

The music teacher, Mrs. Hairel, usually had several children dress in the same type of costume for school plays, but McKay would not agree to other children wearing groundhog costumes for this one. He wanted to be the only groundhog in the play!

◆ McKay didn't grow too old to believe in a Santa Claus who delivered gifts. He enjoyed this particular Christmas with Santa in New York City.

We took limousine rides when we ◆
visited New York City. McKay
was wide-eyed and very happy.
He was amazed at how fast the
taxi drivers drove and vowed to
be a taxi driver when he grew
up! I am grateful that he had fun
moments in his life and that I was
a part of the fun.

This is the telescope McKay put
together. He later broke it when
he fell while carrying it out the
front door. Yet even though he'd
broken the lens, McKay still
gazed through it in awe at the
stars. I, too, look at life as though
through a broken lens. Yet I
remind myself that even though
my vision of life is distorted at
times by the loss of McKay and
his betrayal by someone he loved,
I still need to stand in awe of
what I see and experience. I am
blessed to have learned this from
McKay's example.

◆

◆

Ah, the infamous fruit tray! Delivered
by room service at a hotel at which we
stayed on one trip to New Orleans, the
fruit made McKay sick, likely because he
washed a large amount of it down with
a glass of milk. In attempting to help
McKay to the bathroom, McKay's father
slipped, fell, and slid across the bathroom
floor with McKay in his arms. It sounded
like an explosion when they hit the bathroom wall, but McKay made it through
the ordeal without even a bruise.

♦ McKay and I loved New Orleans—the charm of the old seaport city touched our entire family. One of our favorite stops on our frequent visits was the New Orleans Zoo, where McKay had the opportunity to ride a camel.

Our most wonderful kite-flying experience took place on the Mississippi Gulf Coast. McKay and I had tried many times to fly a kite and had met with minimal success. This particular excursion turned out to be our "lucky day," as McKay called it. That leisurely afternoon of kite flying strengthened the bond between us.

♦

♦

Each person has a unique way of expressing himself. One of McKay's forms of expression was playing music. It was not unusual for McKay to spend time alone each day playing an instrument. I often wondered what he was feeling when he would disappear for long periods of time and play.

♦ Wiley Coyote was with McKay throughout his life. He even went with McKay to church dinners on Wednesday nights for a period of time. I was given Wiley to hold after I was told of McKay's death and during my recovery from the stroke. I still have Wiley.

♦ This is the last photo we took of McKay when he was alive. It was taken the week of McKay's abduction and murder. He was on his way to school with his trusty backpack. I look at this picture and find myself shaking my head in disbelief that all of this happened. I remain baffled as to how anyone can harm a child.

♦ The NOWA (Never Open When Alone) decal was created to remind children never to open the door to anyone when home alone. It instructs them to instead contact a trusted friend or family member or to call 911. The decal is attached at the child's eye level to the inside of all exterior doors in the home.

—Courtesy of The Courier

Hilton Crawford, shown during a death row interview in 1996, was sentenced to death for the abduction and slaying of 12-year-old McKay Everett. 'Uncle Hilty,' as McKay called Crawford, was a longtime friend of the boy's family. The former Beaumont police officer and Jefferson County deputy claimed that another man was responsible for McKay's death.

A boy is killed after being kidnapped for ransom by a friend of the family ... a family that dissolves after the murder of its only child. Their betrayer is scheduled to die July 2 ... to the end, asking for forgiveness that cannot be given.

The Trespasses of Uncle Hilty

The McKay Foundation/www.protectingchildren.org

—Courtesy of The Beaumont(TX) Enterprise.

—Photos courtesy of the Associated Press

CRAWFORD CASE TIMELINE

Samuel McKay Everett

Executed

Continued from Page 1A.

The failed kidnap plot was intended to enable Crawford to pay off personal debts, but the scheme fell apart before the Everetts could take steps to meet the $500,000 ransom demand that was to have produced the payoff.

The crime shocked the region because of its brutality and the betrayal of trust that was at its heart. The onetime friend and neighbor of the Everetts was known as "Uncle Hilty" to his young victim, but Crawford didn't directly mention his victim in his final words.

The execution by injection was deferred for two minutes while Crawford offered a last statement that included thanks to supporters during his stay on Death Row at the state prison in Livingston. But he also turned his head to

Sept. 12, 1995
McKay Everett, home alone while his parents go to an Amway meeting, is missing when his parents return. They get a ransom call and quickly notify authorities.

Sept. 13
Crawford checks into a Beaumont motel in the pre-dawn hours. The FBI enters the case.

Sept. 14
The FBI and Montgomery County deputies impound Crawford's car after visiting him upon his return to Conroe.

Sept. 15
Crawford is arrested for aggravated kidnapping.

Sept. 16
Irene Flores, the accomplice who made the ransom call, is arrested in Houston, also for aggravated kidnapping. Crawford tells authorities McKay is dead and where to find the body.

Sept. 17
Authorities recover McKay's body off Interstate 10 in Louisiana between Lafayette and Baton Rouge.

Sept. 20
More than 1,000 people attend McKay's funeral at First Baptist Church in Conroe. Meanwhile, a grand jury

Hilton Crawford

delivers indictments charging Crawford with capital murder and Flores with aggravated kidnapping.

Sept. 25
Crawford pleads not guilty in state district court in Conroe.

Oct. 20
Crawford's lawyer says her client has implicated others in the kidnap plot, but she won't give names.

Jan. 30, 1996
State District Judge Fred Edwards grants a change of venue for Crawford's trial and shortly picks Huntsville for the site.

July 7
Crawford's murder trial begins.

July 17
Jurors see a video of Crawford admitting a role in the crime but naming "R.L. Remington" as the killer.

July 24
Jurors take one hour to convict Crawford of capital murder. Six days later, they condemn him to death and he is moved to Death Row in Livingston.

Sept. 13
A Montgomery County judge denies Crawford's motion for a new trial.

Feb. 17, 1999
The Texas Criminal Court of Appeals in Austin denies Crawford's appeal.

Dec. 17, 2002
The 5th U.S. Circuit Court of Appeals in New Orleans refuses to hear Crawford's appeal.

Feb. 11, 2003
State District Judge Fred Edwards sets July 2 as Crawford's execution date.

June 23, 2003
The U.S. Supreme Court refuses to take Crawford's case.

July 2, 2003
Crawford is executed.

Pennies from heaven

McKay's pennies help mother recover from tragedy

By Al Greenwood
Courier staff

Paulette Everett always believed in angels, but she says she never had one to watch over her until her son's death three years ago.

McKay, Paulette's son, enjoyed church, playing the piano, reading books and collecting pennies. He started collecting the copper coins when he was in the first grade and continued until his death at the age of 12.

The details surrounding McKay's death still seem fresh in the minds of many Montgomery County residents.

As Paulette recalled, she and husband Carl left town on a business trip Sept. 12, 1995. McKay stayed behind at the family's Conroe home.

Later in the day, Carl called to check on McKay. When their son didn't answer the telephone, Carl rushed home, hoping McKay had simply fallen asleep in front of the TV.

But Carl became frightened when he saw the back door of the house ajar, according to Paulette. "He dashed inside calling for McKay. Then the phone rang. It was someone demanding half a million

Paulette Everett today

show in Atlanta this summer.

"One of his favorite songs was from 'Cats'," Paulette said.

When she entered the convention hall, a pianist started playing that very song. "It was a very, very memorable moment for me. He played it and I cried. He asked me what was wrong, and I told him about McKay."

■ ■ ■

Besides the library, Paulette also works with the Samuel McKay Everett Foundation.

When the Everetts first heard about the ransom, they received several anonymous donations, Paulette said.

"When McKay didn't come home, we really didn't have a way to return each dollar," she said. "We set about then to honor the gifts that were given."

Those donations led to the foundation's birth.

For 1999, the group plans to develop a program to educate families about protecting children from kidnapping, physical abuse and other threats.

The foundation is now trying to send educational materials to each of the 82,500 homes in Montgomery County.

"We have made slow but steady

said. "I wondered, 'How in the world did

—Courtesy of The Courier

♦ I look back now at these news releases, and they give me a strong dose of reality, stirring up painful memories from the past.

Chapter Six: The Trial

Genesis 4:9-10
Then the Lord said to Cain, "Where is Abel your brother?"
And Cain said, "I do not know. Am I my brother's keeper?"
And He said, "What have you done? Your brother's blood is crying to Me
from the ground."

I would sometimes say the verses this way:

Then the Lord said to Hilton Crawford and all the others involved in any way,
"Where is McKay, your brother who loved Me?"
And all those involved said, "I do not know. Am I my brother's keeper?"
And the Lord said, "What have all of you done?
The voice of McKay's blood is crying to Me from the ground."

I remember one day when I sitting on the bench with my sister. During pretrial hearings, the judge was hearing other cases, and I observed a mother standing before the judge for abusing her children and for choosing to do nothing when the father abused the children. I looked at my sister and she said, "In today's world, Mother and Daddy would be before a judge." It was a very sobering moment.

During this time, Carl was surrounded by his buddies. They were his support during a time when I needed him. I try to present Carl and his behavior during all of this in a positive light. Maybe he drew strength from his friends' presence. I really didn't want to be around anyone in particular—except maybe Wayne because he seemed to calm me down. I try to put myself in Carl's shoes and not judge him harshly. Each person is different when walking through hell, but there were times I just wanted Carl to pat me on the back and say he appreciated the mom I was to McKay. I tried to remember to thank him for sincerely loving McKay.

Carl and I were told that the district attorney's office would be questioning people who could possibly give more information concerning Hilton Crawford and the involvement of his family and friends in the abduction and murder of McKay. We had been told that the DA suspected that Connie Crawford, Hilton's wife, had covered for Hilton in other cases of wrongdoing, and also that she had talked with him on the night he had McKay.

Carl and I met in downtown Conroe and went to a taller building that overlooked the front of the DA's office. We found a window that had a view of the street that ran past the office, so we watched and waited. We did not know who they would be questioning, and we wanted to know because we had been under the impression that all the questioning was completed.

We noticed a sports car pull into a parking space in front of the building. It belonged to Hilton's youngest son, Kevin, and we knew then that Kevin would have information about not only his father, but also the rest of his family.

Carl and I left the bank building and ran across the street to the courthouse. We scooted into the lower level parking where prisoners were released and delivered. There was a break in the wall at ground level, and the shrubs that were planted in front of the wall were spaced apart, providing us with an ample view of the office where Kevin was to be questioned.

Carl and I watched as hand gestures grew to fists, and we watched the intense emotions climb to anger. We felt that the questioning must have become threatening to Kevin or he would not have reacted in the manner he did. He left in a storm of feelings, and we watched as he left the building and drove off in his car, anger evident in his body language and driving style. We realized that the DA's office probably hit some nerves. Carl later questioned the DA but received very little information. We continued to be frustrated at the lack of information they shared with us.

Christmas of 1996 was like an ice storm: we put up no tree and we played no music. I couldn't bear to decorate the tree with all of McKay's baby shoes and the other ornaments that held his memories. I don't remember much except going to Houston and staying in a hotel. Carl and I were walking robots. I remember sitting at a monument that paid tribute to those who have had cancer, and I remember reading the inscriptions over and over as I thought of the feelings these people must have experienced during their own ice storms. I did not want to lose touch with the human race and human suffering that all of us have to bear at one time or another.

Hilton's defense wanted to move the trial to El Paso, which is 700 miles from Conroe and has a large Catholic population. They wanted to do this in hopes of avoiding the death penalty. However, it was finally decided that the trial would take place 30 miles north of Conroe in Huntsville, TX.

That year, Carl and I each gave the other a Christmas gift. I remember that it was a first for him to wrap my gifts himself. I don't remember what was underneath the crumpled wrapping paper, but I remember that he cried as he laid them on my lap and walked away. The ill-wrapped packages were a blessing because he had spent the time to wrap them himself. I'm not sure I ever thanked him for the effort, but I did appreciate it. I still remember these packages each Christmas—they are one of my most blessed memories of Carl.

Another beautiful memory of Carl is when I was once home cleaning the bathrooms. When Carl came home and found me, I was scrubbing a toilet. I sat on the floor when he entered the room, and he sat down on the floor with me. He placed the gifts in my lap. It was and is one of the moments in time that I consider most special. We were alone, and he was willing to join me on the floor of the bathroom in order to give me an anniversary gift. Even though this might not sound romantic, it was. For those moments, we shared a bond.

During the pretrial hearings, we heard that Hilton—and possibly Connie— would be charged with some federal offenses. When it was discovered that Hilton's stolen car, a late-model Mercury Marquis, was resting peacefully in a storage shed owned by his friend Billy Allen, the eroded character of Hilton Crawford and his friends began to be exposed. I remember Connie Crawford telling me of the stolen car in the early 1990s. She told me she had placed all of her jewelry in the trunk of her car because she did not trust the maid, and then she told me the car had been stolen from work. I asked her how her car could be stolen from an elementary school parking lot, especially when I knew from past history that Connie parked her car close to the school. She laughingly told me she guessed it was because she had parked her car farther from the school that day. Time passed, and another teacher saw Connie wearing the "stolen" jewelry at school. One fellow teacher remarked about the jewelry and Connie's response was "Well, you know Hilty. He found all my jewelry in a pawn shop in Houston." We were later told by law enforcement that they thought Hilton or Billy Allen had removed the car from the teachers' parking lot. The total of this probable insurance scam was over $55,000.

This scam is one of three that Hilton was suspected of. The second, another case of insurance fraud, involved Hilton breaking a window at his home and reporting a theft of $50,000 worth of jewelry. The third crime he committed was running a horse that was illegal to run in Texas. His history of crime certainly aided in the trial against him.

Investigators also discovered that the storage sheds were used to store not only a stolen vehicle but also the murder weapon: a .45 caliber semiautomatic pistol used on a twelve-year-old child. The blood-drenched trunk mats were burned by Billy Allen, the owner of the sheds. A worker and another man named Gary Capo were in Buna at the storage sheds on the morning after McKay's abduction and murder.

Carl and I drove to the storage sheds in Buna, Texas. It was a cold, rainy day, and we hoped we would happen upon the three men who stood and watched as the bloody evidence burned. I still have a difficult time imagining that three grown men would, simply because they were asked, burn bloody car mats. Why didn't they ask questions? Obviously, some sort of crime had taken place, and these men's silence enabled Hilton Crawford to sink to the lowest form of human being: a murderer. Even though Hilton may have lied to the men about the reason for burning the bloody mats, I in no way excuse these men's behavior, and I believe that whether they burned the mats or simply stood by and watched, they should have been charged with destroying evidence. These three men, if involved in burning evidence, deserved to be charged with third-degree felonies punishable by law from two to ten years. The evidence was burned, and the men were not charged. These men became involved in a tangled web of deception that I hope cost them the respect of fellow citizens, family, and friends.

Carl and I decided to go to Houston to visit with the federal authorities who were housed in the Lyric building. We felt that Hilton should be charged with everything allowable by law, and that an investigation into Connie's involvement was imperative at both the local and federal level. The D.A.'s office did not help push for this to happen. Carl waited in the car because we felt it would be best if I went alone. The lobby of the building was empty, except for a baby grand piano—a nice tie-in to the name of the building. I went to the display board where the names and office numbers were posted, and as I searched for the offices I needed, the piano began to play. I turned around, expecting to see the pianist on the bench, but there was no one playing the electronically operated piano. The tune was "Memory," which made me both cry and smile. This was another moment in time when I knew I had entertained an angel—a perfectly timed, perfectly selected angel for me. A moment of love sent from Heaven. A moment when earthly time comingled with the spiritual. I thought for a moment of the writing of St. Paul when he could not explain what happened—he could only relay the events of what he saw and heard.

I found it difficult to face these authorities whom I did not know, especially because I was visiting them to ask that they prosecute the Crawfords to the fullest extent of the law for prior crime or crimes. I also wanted to tell the authorities of my suspicions concerning others involved. But I did it; I did it for McKay.

When the investigation started, Daryl Fields, the US attorney for the Eastern District of Texas, had come forward wanting to present a charge to the federal grand jury. The charge was dismissed, and he declined to discuss the reasons for the dismissal. The district attorney's office suggested that Carl and I not press for federal charges against the Crawfords—a mistake, in my opinion. I would urge anyone to weigh carefully what you are encouraged to do during a criminal proceeding.

When the jury selection, trial, and sentencing were moved to Sam Houston State University's criminal justice building, I made the decision to try to attend. Carl was working out of town, and I really don't know what motivated me to go up and sit through all the questioning of potential jurors, but I went. The days came and went as I sat through most of the jury selection by myself. I felt old and tired and completely unlike myself. I was a stranger in a foreign land, unsure of my ability to communicate or cope.

One morning when I arrived, Hilton Crawford and I ended up face to face. As he and I sat down at the same time, we ended up glaring into each other's eyes. Hilton cursed me in a whispered voice and I responded, "Good morning." A detective from the district attorney's office who was sitting in the row behind me grabbed me from behind and held me. He pulled me backwards. His face was beside mine. He whispered under his breath, "You can't do that!" I told him that I just said good morning. Apparently, he did not hear Hilton cursing me. Criminals are slick, even in a court of law.

I could see the hate in Hilton's face. I never knew he housed so much contempt for Carl and me; apparently he had kept it well hidden. I looked into the eyes that McKay saw on the night he was killed, and I was not afraid. Hilton's facade hid rage, a rage intense enough to kill a child. (Hilton had been compared to Henry Lee Lucas and Lee Harvey Oswald.) I didn't want to miss this masquerade inside someone's soul again.

During the pretrial hearings, Carl and I drove to Mississippi. We were a sad lot as we looked for a penny all the way home. Every little spot caused us to pause and sadly determine that the spot was not a penny. I remarked to Carl that I hoped he was not upset that McKay was really busy and could not worry with having a penny sent to us.

That evening when we arrived home, Carl turned on the TV in order to hear the news in general, and to get any news that was televised concerning the Hilton Crawford case. When he settled in, the news of a cameraman's death was broadcast. Apparently, this man's van had a blowout, and the man had died. We were devastated, and I remarked that I now knew where McKay was that day. He was waiting to greet the cameraman.

I attended the funeral of the cameraman, and the American Indian music stirred deep feelings in me. I was given a tape of similar music when McKay died. The music was a language all its own, and it spoke only in notes. It spoke of long ago, of a time past, of people who left their mark on our world. The songs were moments of precious memories of a time gone by. I understood this concept.

The cameraman's friends spoke. They laughed and cried. They shared their intimate moments with those who had come to celebrate a life. The wife brought with her a level of respect for her husband. She sang, even though she was not a trained singer. The realness of the service was beyond words.

One night, I could not sleep. It weighed heavily that the cameraman's wife did not know that my McKay was with her husband. I pondered and prayed, and then decided to write my heart. I told her everything. I felt as if I was running the risk of being ridiculed, but I decided that I could not carry my feelings any longer.

Months passed, and I received a note from the cameraman's mother. She relayed that her daughter-in-law had mailed a copy of my letter to her, and she asked if she might share the letter with one of her dear friends. The friend is employed by *Guideposts*, and when she received the letter, she contacted me. I wrote to her as well.

A span of time passed, and I received a copy of the story that I had written, but I found that my words had been edited. I was so disappointed that my writing was not accepted just as it was sent, and my insecurity was at an all-time high. I visited with Wayne about my concerns and told him I was mad and hurt that they did not accept my story as written. Wayne chuckled and said, "It is called editing." I worked through my feelings and decided that it was an honor to share the story, even edited. The general story was the same; the message just as important.

The jury was finally selected, and the trial began. The atmosphere of the trail was paradoxical—so serious, yet with a circus-like excitement created by the swarms of people buzzing everywhere. The trial was not only a time of exposing Hilton, his friends, and his family; it was also a time for me to look inward, realizing that life can bring circumstances that are overwhelming. I carefully listened to what was said and how it was said.

As the trial progressed, and the days blurred into one another, I felt a sting each time I realized that the testimony was revealing an individual whose character had been eroded. I wondered if integrity had ever played a role in Hilton's life and in the lives of those who contributed to the events that shadowed the abduction and murder of McKay. I wondered, as these whitewashed lives were being exposed by questions that revolved around the death of a child, if these people would forever be changed for the better. Or would this crime become no more than a temporary blip on the screen, a point of momentary correction only to be abandoned when the next corrupt money-making scheme arose?

I evaluated my life and the times I could have done better. I thought of the times I would tell my little ones at school: before you point a finger at someone else, look at your own hand—there are three fingers pointing back at you. This was a time of taking a moral inventory of my life, a look inside myself. I saw snippets of myself in bits of the attitude and behavior in some of the unsavory people on the stand. I felt ugly as I realized that I myself was in need of great personal growth. I would never harm a child, but I still saw particles of myself in the thugs who were on trial. I remember thinking, *I'd best sit up, take notice, and sweep my own house.*

I felt as if I were wounded near to death, yet I was still on Earth. It is my belief that if we are still here, we are here to learn. I would pray daily for the strength and emotional stability to hear and see what I needed in order to gain some wisdom about life. I did not want to bypass the opportunity to learn, even in circumstances like these.

The trial became more of a time of learning and self-evaluation than a time of dealing with the judicial system and Hilton Crawford's being punished. I could not control the judicial system and the process that was to unfold, but I could control my willingness to continue to grow. This soul-searching time led me to gain a belief that there is no "neutral" in life. Either we, as humans, are traveling in a positive, proactive direction, or we are in decline. We do not stand still. There are no time-outs.

Carl and I traveled together to the trial each day. Sometimes we were alone, but most of the time a friend or relative was traveling with us. There were times we would pass Connie Crawford along the way, as she was required to appear in Huntsville each day of the trial, even though they did not call her as a witness. The prosecution wanted her there in case they needed her, a tactic that was designed to apply pressure on her to talk. She never did.

Tight security was evident. I didn't know if there were threats that required extra precautions, but the security was definitely present.

I was the first witness. The stiffness returned to my body when they called my name, and I remember being embarrassed about the amount time it took me to reach the witness chair. I had to be helped to my seat.

While on the stand, I was shown the last photo of McKay. I was asked if I recognized the photo of McKay, and I replied, "That's my baby." The questioning was detailed, and began with my story of how Carl and I met Hilton and Connie Crawford. The most important information came when I testified to the fact that Hilton had called on the afternoon of the abduction to determine if I would be attending the Amway meeting. He had also called the week prior to ask the same question.

I wore the old dress that many were calling "out of character" for me. It was old and it was country, but I was comfortable. The questions were basic, general information about McKay and the night he was taken. My voice was extremely slow. After the questioning I was exhausted. I wanted to go home.

Carl testified to the ransom call demanding $500,000 in $100 bills. My insides went weak when he recounted Flores's words: "We have your son. Do not call the police or the boy will be killed." Somewhere in the rest of her message, she cursed.

At times I felt I would die, and remembering Carl's words (printed by the media at the time of McKay's abduction) helped calm me. He had said of McKay: "Even though he might be barefooted at this point in time, he'll walk on thorns to get back home." I remembered the love and devotion the three of us had for each other.

Each day, the boxes containing information and evidence were wheeled into the courtroom. I would count the boxes as I reminded myself that one day I would want to see inside them and discover some of the unknown details surrounding McKay's death.

I didn't read any of the news clippings between the time of McKay's abduction and the end of the trial. A scrapbook of news clippings was kept for me, and at first I thought this was morbid—now I am grateful for the information. I read them for the first time in 2001. I looked at the photos of Hilton Crawford in the newspaper clippings and remembered how he looked during the trial. His eyes were puffy, not just underneath, but all around them. He would quickly glance around when he was entering or exiting a building. Some of the pictures in the newspapers seemed to show a smirk. I covered the eyes and looked at his mouth. Then I would cover the mouth and look at the eyes. I did not see remorse in his face. I have been told that the eyes are the window to the soul. What did I see? Did I see sorrow or "sorry I got caught"?

During the trial, I recognized some of Hilton's clothes. They were not shabby, but they were not new either. I wondered if he missed his nice home and the ability to shop for a new shirt or shoes. I wondered if he dreamed about being free and what he would do if he regained his freedom. I wondered if he thought of swimming in his pool with his faithful dog.

The sketch artists interested me. I wondered if the drawings would reveal the demons within Hilton Crawford and his friends. I often looked back and forth between the men and their illustrated faces. I wanted the people who viewed the sketches on TV to know without a doubt that these men were "walking evil." I wanted there to be no doubt that Hilton's heart was dead, and I wanted it to show in the sketches. I didn't want any of us to miss these demons again.

I asked myself over and over, *What did I miss? What didn't I see?* It was a daily beat-myself-up time. Mothers and daddies are supposed to protect their children. We are supposed to sense danger. I did sense it, and my alarms were going off, but I did not know what to do.

I visited with one sketch artist, and she told me that a friend had been murdered, and she, the artist, had done the sketches at her friend's murderer's trial. This artist was a great lady of courage. She was a solace to me.

At court, Connie was nowhere to be found. I knew she had come to court because we passed her most days on the highway to Huntsville, but she wasn't in the courtroom. I decided to find her, so I began on the side of the building where I had not walked when I needed to stretch my legs. I quietly looked in each room until I came to a room where I noticed a human shape against the windows. The room was unlit, and I did not enter. I just stared silently. It was Connie. My friend held my arm and urged me not to enter the room. I wondered if Connie could feel my presence and the thousand questions that I wanted to ask. "Why didn't you help on the night McKay was taken? Why did you cover for Hilton on September 12?"

I wanted to strangle the truth out of her. There are times when I regret not putting my hands around her neck and demanding the answers, but I knew if I did, I would be perceived as the "bad" person. Connie Crawford had done a great job of portraying herself as the "dumb" wife . . . the "dumb" wife who would not take a polygraph, who did not know how to pump gas. This concept of Connie did not fit with her well-hewn organizational skills. Like oil and water, these two personalities she was trying to combine don't mix.

Finally, she turned towards me like a robot, and I saw a person whom I no longer knew. A greater reality for me was that I probably never knew her. I felt no emotion from her. She stared for a while, but we did not speak. She turned slowly back toward the window and looked out. I knew then that she was either not alive emotionally, or she had a remarkable ability to detach herself from reality.

At one point during the trial, Connie requested that Carl call her. Our attorney asked that Carl call her back from his office so he could listen in and record the conversation. Carl agreed. I remember that when Carl asked Connie why Hilton hurt McKay, she said it was because McKay got too loud. Somewhere in the conversation, Connie Crawford said, "Carl, I'm not going to desert you, Honey." I remember Carl being so hurt and taken aback by her lack of emotion during the conversation. She stated everything in a matter-of-fact way.

I sat inside and outside the courtroom. If the testimony began to make my body feel stiff and my speech began to slur, I would exit the courtroom and sit in the lobby or stand on the outside balcony. I would try to pray, although my verbal usage of language was weak. I knew what I felt, and I did not know how to talk with a God that would allow such a crime against a child. Praying had become a conversation with a God I did not know or like. I felt like a child whose best friend had been a traitor. I admit I did not know how to pray in circumstances like these. I felt helpless and hopeless. My flesh felt burned, and my nerve endings were giving me trouble, especially in my legs.

I continued with therapy, and Vernon, my therapist, attended the trial whenever possible. He knew a lot about McKay from past therapy sessions, and he could see that the stress level for me was mounting. He did what be could to lighten the mood in court. One time, he brought blue M&Ms and proceeded to eat them one at a time, right out of his shirt pocket. I had told Vernon the story of the day McKay realized that M&Ms came in blue. We had thrown a celebration and tasted the blue ones to determine if they tasted any different that the rest. We licked them to see what our tongues would look like with the blue color on them, and we figured the ratio of blue to the rest of the bag or to the different colors. I relish those moments with McKay in celebrating the simple pleasures of life, and I'll remember the one who honored those simple moments by caring enough to bring a box of M&Ms to court.

During preparation for the trail, I had requested to be absent during certain testimony. I had heard testimony about a fracture to the bone just below McKay's left eye socket, indicating that he had been hit in the face, probably with a tire iron. On the day in court when this evidence was presented, I had intended to be absent, but before I knew it, the facts were being presented and it was too late for me to leave. My soul aches as I recall the testimony that brought to light the struggles McKay had experienced during his capture. There were marks in the trunk of the car that proved that McKay rode in the trunk while alive and struggling to be free.

There was still a question in the case; there was an indentation on the rim of the trunk that fit the form of a flashlight. I wondered if the flashlight had been in the trunk and whether McKay had shone it in the eyes of the killer when he opened it. However, the flashlight was never found. It was thought that it was probably removed from the home when things were seen being moved out.

During the day of that testimony, when the expert witness had uttered about two sentences into the details, my emotions began to seep out like the steam from a tea kettle. A scream slowly eked out. Later, those nearby said it began as little squeaky sounds then slowly climbed to a crescendo scream. My emotions exploded. I remember screaming and screaming, even though I did not recognize the sounds as coming from me. I was later told I screamed for three straight minutes. The courtroom became noisy, and people began to leave. Judge Fred Edwards pounded and pounded his gavel and said, "Order in the court! Order in the court!" Hilton Crawford turned slowly and looked at me. Our eyes met, and his eyes were lifeless, void of emotion.

One of Carl's friends jumped over his seat in order to help my mother, and Carl came to help me from where he had been sitting with his friends. The judge began to yell, "Clear the courtroom! Clear the courtroom!" Carl and my sister helped me to the car. It was an odd time for me to laugh, but that is what I did when I was riding home. It wasn't a laugh of fun; it was a laugh of release. Carl became frustrated by my laughter. He first thought I had screamed on purpose, but I told him I hadn't. Hilton's lawyer later tried to ask for a mistrial due to my scream, but the judge denied the request.

Vernon said it was the most real I had been since McKay's abduction. He did suggest I communicate again with the district attorney's office so I'd be forewarned about any testimony that could ignite a scream. I did as he suggested, and I also decided to take a little break from the courtroom. I did not mind sitting in peace and quiet and being away from information that caused me so much emotional, mental, and physical pain.

For the next few days after the scream I slept well. The local therapist called Wayne and told him to be ready to help with me if necessary; Wayne didn't come to help me unless I asked him to. He didn't go to court except during the sentencing phase.

Vernon said I was doing better than before I screamed—an effective emotional catharsis. I look back on those moments, and I can feel myself in the courtroom. That moment in time is one I can revisit with such realness that I get angry each time I think of it. In mind, I can go back in time to the point where the squeaks are coming out of me, and my eyes meet the eyes of the witness. My wish is that I could return to some of my moments with McKay with the same intensity. I had been reading *The Primal Scream* when the trial began. On the day I screamed, I was in the third chapter. I decided I would put the book away for a while.

My rage and anger turned to words like idiot, stupid, and dumb. There was no way a plan such as this would have succeeded. No one with even a shadow of involvement or knowledge could have hoped to pull off the crime. I shake my head and wonder how these people could be so shortsighted and lacking in common sense and compassion. They had given no thought to, *What if this doesn't work? What if I get swept away? What if God chooses to look upon this act as Sodom and Gomorrah and rain down fire and brimstone judgment in the form of prison? Then what will I do?* Why did so many insist on attempting this horrifying chain of events that had NO chance of success?

My question to Hilton and Flores (the woman who made the ransom call) would be : "Was it worth it? Was it worth the price you have had to pay, Hilton? Flores, is it worth the price you are paying?" I would ask those who covered for Hilton, his friends, and his family: "Is it worth the price you have had to pay? What now for your life? What are all of you doing today that counts for something? Do you still hide weapons and stolen property? Do you still cover the wrongdoings of others and enable them to continue down a destructive path? Do you still have loose moral boundaries? Do you still have guilt, or did you ever feel guilty, or are you crocodiles in human skin? Do you have a guilt that requires protection under the Fifth Amendment? Do you realize that something so simple as driving a person to use a pay phone can turn your life into a shambles?"

The female who drove Flores to the pay phone to make a ransom call claimed protection under the Fifth Amendment. What kind of a person would assist in a ransom call?

The silence in my home snuffed out my denial. There was no way around the fact that McKay was not only missing, he was dead. I had been catty about denial, saying things like, "Denial is a wonderful thing—sometimes it is all you've got." Now, reality for me is a moment-by-moment struggle to accept life without McKay.

During the trial, I could see that Hilton's friends and family were still in denial about his being a child murderer. Some of them even verbalized their disbelief after the trial; they said they had come because they needed to hear proof that he was guilty. I am amazed that it took the long walk through the legal process for his friends and family to accept his guilt. Their denial was set in cement!

I drank lots of diet drinks, and people began to notice. The one thing they could do for me was replace my warming Diet Coke with a cooler one from the drink machine. I developed an addiction to caffeine . . . or should I say a *stronger* addiction to caffeine. Since high school, I had used iced tea in the mornings to wake up, and now I was drinking between six and ten diet drinks a day. Vernon said he was happy I was not a drinker of alcohol because I would be a candidate for a drinking problem. I decided that after the trial I would address my overindulgence in diet drinks because of health issues, including the sodium causing me to retain water.

Carl and I were also eating more; we both gained weight. Twenty extra pounds added to my small frame had nowhere to hide; even my neck was thick. I wore loose-fitting clothes and lots of warm-up suits to hide the extra weight. Another physical side effect of grief began to wear me down—excess weight.

During the trial, Carl and I ate lunch together. One day, our attorney joined us, and we asked him if we might drive to the prison facility where Hilton would be taken if convicted of capital murder. He was willing to drive us, and when we arrived at the Ellis Unit, we noticed it was a massive masonry building surrounded by fencing and razor wire. Our attorney asked if we would like to go inside, and we told him we thought we would benefit from seeing where Hilton would reside. Our attorney walked to the guard post and asked if we could have a tour of death row. The guard cleared our entry, and we placed our driver's licenses in a container, which was pulled up to the guard. A female prison escort was sent to give us a tour.

The guard explained the layout of the prison, and the schedule an inmate follows while there. The facility was old, and inmates were walking the corridors. I cannot say I felt fear, but I quickly noticed that the demeanor of some of the inmates reminded me of the bad boys on the junior high and high school campus. Most of us were glad when bad guys dropped out of school, because if they remained in school, they were capable of harming other students.

As we walked the corridors, the guard explained where Hilton would be housed. The cells were on our left, and the windows were on our right. Immediately upon entering the corridor, to the left was a shower; each inmate showered individually for safety reasons. A TV with poor reception was on a rack that rested above eye level in the corridor on the window side. In the middle of the corridor was a cage with a stainless steel table with two benches attached. The benches had no legs. We were told that inmates were allowed to visit with their attorney in these cages.

Each cell contained a toilet, sink, and a large stainless rack with no legs—legs could be used as weapons. This rack served as a bed frame, and held simply a mattress and a pillow. I stuck my head into an empty cell, and the guard told me it was safe to go inside. I had hesitated, thinking any movement might cause the cell door to close. I realized while standing in the small quarters that Hilton had forfeited a lot trying to get more. This was no beautiful home with a pool and a spa in a spacious backyard. There would be no friendly dog to greet him at the door when he arrived home from work. There would not be a game room with a soft sofa in decorator fabric.

The floor of the corridor was littered with food, empty containers, paper, and excrement. Our attorney stumbled on a shampoo bottle strewn about in the recently thrown debris. It took him a few moments to regain his composure, and he was ready to leave the prison shortly thereafter. I could not help but smile when I think about what a sight we must have been while strolling down death row.

The guard shared with us that the inmate who had littered the corridor would now have all his meals blended together and baked in a loaf pan. As punishment for littering, this "Ellis Loaf," would be his meal. I was later told that the prisoners don't mind the Ellis Loaf because they can munch on it for a while, and the inmates look upon the loaf as if it were a bag of potato chips.

I had told myself to look past the eyes of the inmates, but one inmate had some of the bars on his cell covered up and his skin was so white I could not help but look into his eyes. Curiosity got the best of me. I looked. He stared back at me and said, "You perty," in a childish voice. I asked the guard later how many of the inmates were diagnosed as mentally retarded. She became frustrated with me and said, "Only one." She told me his name and what he had done. The others were apparently well enough to account for their wrongs.

We were shown the office area of the guards. Some of the typewriters were manual, and one had a key missing. An inmate had once removed the key and used the arm attached to it as a weapon against a guard.

I left that day, forever changed. As I became more and more aware of the horror that can enter the life of a child, I felt more the beginnings of a commitment that, to this day, has not wavered: a commitment to stand up for children and their plight against those who would harm them. I came to believe that if a child can be taught to read, write, and do mathematics, then he can be taught about being safe. Children are not born knowing that two plus two equals four. They have to be taught. Why have we, as a society, danced around the issues that plague our children? Is it our own issues that hinder us from taking courage and standing tall for the small voices that are seldom heard?

I have reflected many times on the lies that were used to cover for Hilton Crawford. A person who will lie for a murderer is enabling him to commit wrongdoing. No logical, moral human being could or would cover a violent crime for another human being, no matter the circumstances. Many times in life, we face the temptation to lie in order to cover some hurtful events and to protect the innocent, but in the end, the truth surfaces, and a lot of time and energy spent in covering the truth has been wasted.

The number of lies Hilton Crawford told or asked people to tell seemed endless. He asked two of his employees to lie for him about his whereabouts on the night McKay was abducted. He lied about the time he checked into a hotel in Beaumont after leaving McKay's body in Louisiana. He lied about the theft of his car. He lied about how far he had driven while he said he was dropping by manufacturing plants in East Texas. He lied about killing McKay. He was a liar.

Billy Allen, the owner of the storage sheds in which evidence was hidden, said, "Basically, I told the truth, but I didn't tell all of it that first time." I cannot imagine being married to a man who would stoop to this level. A man who would drink champagne after destroying evidence in a child's murder is a low-life, in my opinion. I found out later that these men were told an elaborate lie by Hilton, and that's why they agreed to burn and hide evidence. But I'm angry because as soon as they heard that Hilton was a suspect in a child's murder, they should have spoken up. They did not. As it turns out, Allen had helped hide Hilton's stolen car and jewelry when he committed insurance fraud.

When I looked at Hilton's family members—his wife and sons—I tried to evaluate their motives for covering for Hilton's wrong. There had to be a reason! Hilton's youngest son even remarked that they were all spoiled by Hilton and that Hilton gave them what they wanted. Would that be motive enough to withhold information or assistance on the night McKay was taken? Why would anyone refuse to help a small child in a life-and-death situation? Why would any family member or friend refuse to give a phone number to a frantic parent or to the authorities?

The various lies Hilton Crawford's family, friends, and employees initially told authorities took a toll on Carl and me. It was difficult not to confront these people when we practically rubbed shoulders with them in the lobby outside the courtroom. At one point, I could no longer stomach their lies. It made me sick to look in their faces and know they had lied, and that their lies had cost McKay his life. I hoped with all my heart that they were at the height of embarrassment, and I knew more than likely that as soon as the trial was over, they would slither back under some rock where they belonged.

In today's world, the computer, as well as the cell phone, had become a great asset in criminal investigations. As it turns out, Hilton had his beeper and Connie's cell phone with him in addition to his own cell phone. Cell phone records are like DNA: highly traceable. While Hilton did not own up to calling home on the night he had McKay, the cell phone records revealed all of his calls. Hilton had called Irene Flores, Billy Allen, and his home that night. The trial transcript describes in detail how the cell phone records were used to determine the route Crawford used the night of McKay's abduction. The cell phone records also prove that Hilton Crawford called his residence four times and twice stayed on the line long enough to have spoken to someone.

Billy Allen testified that Connie Crawford may have held back information as well. Billy said that his wife had called him on his mobile phone before Hilton showed up that night at the storage business. Billy's wife told him that Hilton had called looking for him. Billy testified that he tried to reach Hilton at home, and when he talked with Connie, she gave him a phone number where her husband could be reached. (Reported in the *Houston Chronicle*, July 11, 1996). It's suspicious that Connie didn't know Hilton's phone number on the night that McKay was abducted, but during the cover-up time, she readily gave the contact information to Billy.

The *Chronicle* also reported on July 11, 1996, that, "Evidence has mounted in the criminal trial indicating that Allen, the Crawfords, and possibly others withheld information. McKay lay in a swamp for days, decomposing, while certain individuals had knowledge that might have saved him or helped get his body recovered sooner."

The most staggering information came when a real estate agent testified that she had shown the Crawfords property in Bentwater, an upscale neighborhood on Lake Conroe. The Crawfords indicated on a form that they would be needing a house within three months. Hilton and Connie Crawford were interested in a $290,000 house.

Two weeks later—two weeks before McKay was killed—Crawford called the real estate agent back and asked how much it would cost to add a bar and a bathroom to the 3,200-square-foot house they were interested in. I began to realize that planning the crime to abduct and murder McKay was much like planning a yearly family vacation. The added benefit to this vacation was that there would be a new home purchased shortly after returning home.

❧

The jury returned on July 19, 1996, after only sixty minutes of deliberation, and handed down a sentence of guilty of capital murder. I thought I could hear McKay's voice in the verdict, and Carl and I left the courtroom.

The sentencing phase, which is separate from the trail in Texas, began. Much of the same information was rehashed, and many people tried to testify that Hilton Crawford should not receive the death sentence. It made me sick. Finally, the jurors were dismissed to make their decision. I knew the day would come, and it finally did. I was unsure if everyone on the jury would agree that Hilton Crawford should receive the death penalty. I had learned that life is not predictable, so I did not set my heart on Hilton Crawford's dying in a Texas prison by lethal injection, but I took comfort in the fact that no matter how he eventually died, he would be answering to the Almighty Judge of this universe. I found peace in knowing that whether he died of lethal injection, of a heart attack, at the hands of other inmates, or simply of old age, there would come a point of accountability far greater than any we could administer on earth.

On July 24, 1996, the jury handed down the death penalty for Hilton Crawford.

During a court trial, after the death penalty has been invoked, there is an opportunity for a victim's impact statement. Carl and I agreed that I would speak after the sentencing. I watched Hilton Crawford as I read my statement, and he showed no emotion, just as he had remained stoic during the reading of the jury's decisions.

VICTIM IMPACT STATEMENT

What would I have you remember? There is no reason to speak unless you remember. My words will be lost, floating with no authority, unless they are anchored in your memory and in your hearts. I am not the same person and neither are you, neither is Hilton, and neither is McKay. I am forever changed. I can't go back to square one, neither can you, Hilton, or McKay. I can only tell you of McKay.

McKay was as special as any child. He saw life and this earth through the eyes of a child. If we allow ourselves permission, we too can see life through these eyes. McKay was busy, but he enjoyed his time alone. At night, he would tell us to put on his music. That music evolved over the years from lullabies, to Kermit the Frog, to classical, to whatever it is teenagers like. He even liked Dino, Ray Boltz, Whitney Houston, and Celine Dion.

As a small child, McKay was inspired by Dino's piano playing. One night, the television stage was all decorated in a piano, flowers—everything, and Dino was dressed in white clothes. McKay turned to me and said, 'Woman, you've never matched me up like that!"

McKay enjoyed his pets—three dogs, three cats, and three rabbits. The last rabbits were named Martin, Coretta, and Selena. He was greatly disturbed by Selena's death. He didn't seem to know where or how to make sense of the violence.

McKay loved people—adults as well as children. He loved unconditionally. Being an only child can be lonely, and his time with other people was special to him. I want to thank any adult who was a positive influence on my child's life. Any adult who stooped down to eye level and looked into his beautiful blue eyes and gave him a listening ear. Thank you. Many of McKay's friends touched my life. I do not and did not know all of his friends and the friends' names. I apologize in advance if I omit you.

Chad and Bud: Thank you for being McKay's best buddies. Best friends are special. Sometimes they change, but for McKay's life you always were willing to allow him a time to lead, to help try to build one of his projects; and because he was busy and talkative, you guys helped him know what page the teacher was on.

Zak: Remember the barbershop in the attic? After building it, you gave each other a neat haircut.

Jack and Buddy: Thank you for encouraging McKay to try sports. Your gentle nudging helped him try baseball and football.

Trent and Angela: Thank you both for being like a brother and sister to McKay. Your household taught him how to express all of his emotions.

Heather, Liz, and Cody: Thank you for allowing McKay to participate in your family activities.

Hunter and Krista: Thank you for helping McKay design and dig me a wonderful area for my bench.

Tempranj and Lawford: Thank you for allowing McKay to be your "big brother."

Elizabeth: Thank you for going to the sock hop and for allowing McKay the enjoyment of talking on the phone for hours. I should say, "Thank you, John and Connie," Elizabeth's parents.

Kristin: Thank you for understanding what it is to be an only child.

Lauren: Thank you for showing McKay he could have a friend who wasn't a boy. Your hoop earrings threw him for a whirl. He thought you might not be a tomboy anymore.

McKay was the light of my life. The love and relationship we enjoyed was one-of-a-kind, once-in-a-lifetime. Every day was special with McKay. The most wonderful days of my life were spent with McKay. He always made me feel like Cinderella. So girls, when you called or when he called you, I understood. It was special to have even a little time with McKay.

I do not have an answer for Hilton's actions. I cannot speak for Hilton. I try to imagine what McKay would say to Hilton if he were here to speak. Words fail me. Silence speaks at my house.

I hope McKay's last words will forever sound in Hilton's ears. I know McKay angered Hilton by his words. I know my son fought for his life.

McKay taught me to live in the moment: to enjoy the clouds, nature, a walk, tuna fish, and peanut butter. He had the gift of making the simplest of things beautiful. I realized this long before he died. Many days Carl and

McKay heard me say, 'Today, I am Cinderella!"

I have no answers. I only try to walk in faith knowing that McKay is safe and, as King David said, I will join him one day.

We all need to guard our hearts, our thoughts, and our souls. We need to face all that is dark—don't run. Face it or it will conquer you.

In my own words, I, Paulette Everett, am struggling.

There were hands to shake. There were many people to thank. There were tears and smiles. Carl and I exited the back of the building. We stopped on the top step and looked across the sky ... and saw a rainbow.

Will you have faith in Him that He will return your grain
and gather it from your threshing floor?
—Job 39:12

Chapter Seven
1996: Reality and Healing

After the trial, I thought that life might return to some semblance of the past. It did not. I would crater when I allowed myself to think of what McKay had endured. Life was a waltz with insanity.

From the thoughts I had earlier—that I needed to do something to help other children—the community, friends, and I had decided in 1995 to establish the Samuel McKay Everett Foundation, later to be shortened to The McKay Foundation. The initial monies came from the donations sent for the ransom demand. The Foundation board began planning a Family Field Day for September 2, 1996. The focus of the field day was safety, and it was centered around the family unit. I wasn't much help during the planning for the event. I attended the planning meetings, but I was only a person occupying a chair.

During the event, held at Montgomery County Community College, I felt as if I were going to lie down and die. The opening of the Library Corner for Children was part of the ceremony. There is a fountain at the entrance of the college, and I sat there and listened to the water instead of being in the crowds of people. When I felt I could not go any further without folding up, I left and drove to the nearest Wal-Mart store where I held onto a buggy and walked until I felt I could return to the college. The event was well attended, and it was repeated the following year.

I continued therapy, but during the trial, Vernon had recommended I spend time away at intensive grief therapy. I asked him, "How much more intensive can all of this get?" I asked him for some suggestions on choosing a therapist, and he recommended three locations for the therapy: California, Arizona, and Tennessee. He provided information on all three, and after reviewing each center, I chose Dr. Don Doyle in Germantown, Tennessee.

The need for intensive therapy came from my returning to the fetal position when stressed. I was stuck. I could not seem to move on through my grief. I was extremely stressed during every moment of every day. The quietness of my home was more than I could bear. Each day, my body would begin a decline as the afternoon approached. My afternoon schedule had always included spending time one-on-one with McKay, and during these hours now, I continued to be filled with such intense grief that I could not function.

I would wander around the house trying to keep myself together. I usually found myself on the floor in the fetal position with drool running down the side of my face. I was in a zoned-out state in which I would simply float among my emotions and groan. During this period of time, I had a lady who would help clean house and do laundry. Once, I came out of my zoned-out time to find I was surrounded by teenage girls I did not recognize. The maid had become concerned and sent for her daughters to come and just watch me as I lay on the floor. When I first saw them, I wondered if angels were watching me.

The intense therapy was to help me move more quickly through my grief. I was willing to give it a try, as I did not want to spend the remainder of my days in a dazed, drooling position on the floor, nor did I want to revert back to rocking back and forth like I did after McKay's death.

When I could not bear to deal with one more bit of information, I would rock back and forth. A friend came to visit once, and she was directed to the sofa where I sat rocking back and forth. She sat down to visit, and after a while, she began to rock with me. My voice was very slow when I asked her why she was rocking. She said, "I don't know." We laughed. She is a friend who, without trying, can usually make me laugh.

The rocking back and forth reminded me of Job from the Bible. I had read Job for thirty days prior to McKay's death. I had remarked to Wayne that I hated the book of Job from the Bible. He told me that should be an indication that I needed to plant myself in Job for a period of time until I could come to grips with what I hated about Job. I respected Wayne's opinion and set about reading Job every day for thirty days. The period of rocking in my life brought me to a deep spiritual awareness that is unique to me. Little did I know I would become like Job. I fully accept that Job was a real man who suffered unspeakable loss.

Someone else might see it differently, and that is okay, but for me the rocking caused me to think of Job in the ash heap scraping his boils. He was wanting relief, and he scraped over and over. I wanted relief, and I rocked over and over. I had just enough psychology courses to remember that repeated behaviors and actions bring a feeling of safety and security. I told myself, *You might not know what information about McKay's suffering and death is coming next, but you do know what you are going to do. You are going to rock. You can control that. I can choose to rock; then I will know what will be happening next.*

I did tell myself that the rocking was not the best thing for me to do at a time like this. I knew that my life was not in my own hands, and I did not want to be sent to a psychiatric hospital. I racked my brain as to what I could do that would be repeated behavior without appearing to be a mentally and emotionally disturbed person. I knew I needed another behavior I could substitute for the rocking. Finally, I thought of chewing gum! I asked for someone to get me some gum, and as I began to chew, I stopped rocking. It worked, but then some criticized me for chewing gum in public places. I just couldn't please everyone.

I could not find a substitute, more appropriate behavior for the fetal position: right leg dragging, left arm pulling, and the drooling when I would feel the loss of McKay. I made plans and convinced myself I could go to Germantown, Tennessee, alone. I was desperately trying to gain physical stamina, confidence, and the ability to do something by myself. Over the years, my world had gotten smaller and smaller. Carl had once seen an injured person in Houston, so out of fear he had requested I not drive in the Houston area. Then he heard of problems at the shopping mall and requested I not go shopping without him. Both of us reacted with fear, and I drove less and less. My world became the town where we lived, and I knew it was time for that to change. I could no longer keep Carl comfortable.

I had made a promise to myself when I was immobile and speechless. Each time I saw Wayne's straight back, I would say, "I am going to get me a straight back when I get going again!" I had respect and admiration for the way he carried himself. I had carried so much baggage in my life, and I walked with a stoop in my shoulders. I wanted my slumped shoulders GONE! I also made a promise to myself that I was going to therapy until the therapist told me that I did not have to come anymore. I wanted to regain my independence.

One of my first opportunities to work on getting a straight back was getting to and from therapy in Germantown, Tennessee. I went in September, 1996. I made my reservations, packed my bags, and was off to therapy. When I arrived at the Memphis Airport, I made my way to the car rental area in order to pick up a rental car. While there, I was told I could not rent a car because my license had expired. Another fallout from the chaos and confusion. I had allowed my driver's license to expire.

I was under a time constraint because I could not go to the apartment that was reserved for me until later in the afternoon, after checkout time for the previous clients. I was too early for the apartment, and my license had expired. I could not rent a car. I decided to locate the taxi stand at the airport just in case I had no success in getting the decision at the rental place reversed. I tried to call Carl, but reached his voice mail on his mobile phone. I left him

172

a message about the dilemma, and I told him I would be okay because the airport had food, air conditioning, magazines, and a bathroom. I told him I would remain there until I heard from him or until it was time for me to take occupancy of the apartment. I found a place to sit in front of the pay phones and waited for Carl to return my call. The area was also near the front of the airport, one level above the taxi stand. I sat with my back to the pay phones and read a magazine, but while I was reading, I had a feeling of uneasiness. At first, I thought it was a wave of grief crashing in, but my inner alarm began to sound. I felt as if I were not safe; I felt someone was staring at me. I raised my eyes from the magazine, and there was a man looking right at me. He chuckled when I looked him in the eyes. After making eye contact with me, he quickly left through the doors on my right. I assumed he was laughing at someone else, maybe someone behind me using a pay phone.

I resumed reading my magazine, but ten minutes later, the feeling of being unsafe returned. This time it was stronger. I looked up and again the same man was standing about eight feet in front of me. When my eyes met his, he chuckled louder than before. We stared at each other, and he turned quickly and left as he had done before. His fast stride was one of confidence. This time I turned to look behind me and there was no one using the pay phones, and no one was sitting or standing behind me.

There are no words to tell anyone how I felt that day. I had told Carl that I felt that Hilton's family and friends had viewed McKay as the vulnerable one in our family. With him gone, they would now focus any aggression on me because I would be considered the weaker of the two of us. Sirens were going off inside my head as I realized I had been followed to Memphis by someone who wanted to frighten me. I wasn't sure of the motivation for this man's behavior, but I felt it had something to do with the intense pressure that was being placed on Connie Crawford to come forward with information. To this day, I don't know why Connie had continued to refuse to talk about that night, but I know that she was still being asked questions by law enforcement. I can only guess that the continued questioning was causing stress, and that this man was supposed to frighten me into dropping it. I began to plan what I would do if the man returned a third time.

My plan was to run for the cab stand, get a ride to the apartment, and tell the people who were there what I was dealing with and that I needed a safe place. As I was laying my plans—and thinking irrationally—I should have instead found a security guard and asked for help. Unfortunately, my trust factor with security companies was at an all-time low since Hilton Crawford had worked for a security company. I decided that if the frightening man returned for a third time, I would run to the cab stand and go to Germantown.

Recently, I was watching TV and was changing channels when I came upon a program where a woman was being chased in the daylight. The man chasing her pinned her to a wall and made verbal threats with that sick smile and laugh that I knew so well. I stood in front of the TV, frozen, wondering why the script for this actress had not called for her to scream at this moment. The people walking by didn't notice her circumstances, and she was being threatened right there in broad daylight. I turned the channel realizing that I did not scream, nor did I begin to hold this man responsible for scaring me until six years later when I saw through the fog and realized he may have been working for Billy Allen. It would stand to reason that this should have been investigated, but it never was.

For a third time, the feeling came over me. This time it was with a sick stomach, because I knew I was in jeopardy. He was there when I looked up. I had gathered my belongings close to me, and when our eyes met, he laughed, turned on his heels, and quickly left through the same door for the third time. I grabbed my stuff and ran downstairs to the cab stand. I got in a cab and left the airport, not knowing how far it was to Germantown or where the apartment was located. I had no map.

The cab driver drove out of the airport, and I breathed a sigh of relief. We drove and drove, and at some point, I saw an exit marked Get Well Road. I realize now that some of the things I called signs and wonders may have been called that out of desperation, but no matter what the motivation, I looked at that sign and took it for what it was worth and thought, *I am on the right track. I am going to get well.* I began to notice that we were passing cotton fields and cows. It had been a long time since I had seen a field of cotton. I remembered walking through them as a kid. Once, when I was having an artsy moment I asked Carl to drive me to a harvested field, and I picked some of the empty branches and put them in brown glass snuff bottles for Christmas presents. There is something about the South and the simple elements that create the most memorable moments, like an old cotton gin combing the cotton free of tangles and seeds. I can still recall the rhythm and the relaxing feeling it caused within me as I watched from a distance on hot, summer afternoons during childhood.

The elderly black cab driver, who reminded me of Hoke in *Driving Miss Daisy*, drew me out of my reverie when he said "Missus, I know you think that I'm bringing you out to the middle of nowhere to do you bodily harm, but you are all right with me. I know right where you need to go."

In my head I said, "Sweet Jesus, I came here to get help!" I could only hope that someone on this crazy earth could be trusted. The driver came to a stop in front of a row of apartments. He had honored what he had said. I went into the apartment and told the lady cleaning that I needed to be in the apartment early. The woman was Dr. Doyle's wife. I told her of my dilemma and that I needed to get some groceries for the apartment. I asked her if she could help me, and she took me to the grocery store and helped me get settled. As she left me, she motioned to a notebook on the table and told me I would need to get started on my homework. I nodded a yes.

I bolted the door, settled in, and began the process of intensive therapy. After asking myself more than once what in the world I was doing in intensive therapy, and why in the world had God allowed such horror and chaos in McKay's life, the phone rang. The female on the other end of the line asked me if I needed a chimney sweep. I told her that the place where I was staying was not my own so I did not know if the owner would need a chimney sweep.

I thought that it was a strange call, but I did know of areas in the US that did have need of chimney sweeps. Out of nowhere, the female asked me if I knew Sam Petro. Sam Petro was Hilton Crawford's best friend. I know now that the man in the airport and the phone call were connected.

I was silent and began to think. I told myself to keep this woman on the line long enough to hopefully be able to trace the call. I also told myself to be honest because honesty is the best policy. I told the person on the other end of the line that I did not know a Sam Petro in Tennessee, but I did know a Sam Petro in The Woodlands, Texas. The person on the other end of the phone became very quiet, and there were several seconds of silence. I felt as if someone was in the room coaching her on what to ask next. The next question was, "Are you in a house or an apartment?"

I asked myself if I wanted to be truthful about this answer. I chose truthfulness and said that I was in an apartment. This phone call confirmed that the man in the airport was without a doubt sent, but sent to do what? The phone caller had tried to frighten me. It did not work. I became very angry and determined to move forward in life with an intensity that would intimidate whoever had called me.

I think it was disarming to the caller because I did not panic. I kept her on the phone as long as I could. As soon as she hung up, I called my sister Patsy, who was three hours away in Mississippi, and asked her how quickly she could get from Jackson to Memphis. She said if she drove fast it would take about three hours.

I asked her to bring me a gun if I called her back. I told her what had happened and that I was in jeopardy being by myself. I called Carl again and finally reached him. I told him what had happened and that I needed some help.

I called Dr. Doyle and told him I did not have time for him to psychoanalyze me, but that I needed to know that I could receive some help if necessary. I called the local police and the Memphis police, but I was told that because I wasn't hurt, they could not do anything.

Carl called back, and then he contacted the district attorney's office and the FBI. We were both puzzled as to how anyone had gotten the phone number to the therapist's apartment. Carl and I had not shared the information with anyone. The FBI and district attorney's office retraced the events and decided that the woman who called had gotten the number by listening to Carl's mobile phone. Carl had called the apartment trying to find me when he received my phone call about my driver's license. Dr. Doyle's wife had answered the phone and had spoken with Carl. This is when the FBI thinks the caller retrieved the phone number at the apartment.

Carl could not get a flight out to Memphis that evening, so he chartered a flight. He spent the week in Memphis so I would not be alone.

On the first day of therapy, I forced the issue with Carl that he needed to meet Dr. Doyle. I told him I did not want to fight the battles with him over who was trying to help me. I was over the need to keep secrets in life, and I needed help and he needed to be a responsible husband and at least meet Dr. Doyle. He finally agreed, and he met Dr. Doyle.

Dr. Doyle's sessions started early in the morning. When Carl and I arrived, we entered his office area, and the music was at a very "nice" volume. The "Hallelujah Chorus" was in full sound. There was no lunch break, and most of what was in his refrigerator was healthy—water and fruit juice. He calls what we did in intensive therapy GOIN' SANE. I asked him if he had worked with very many families who had lost children through acts of murder. He told me that the closest to working with people suffering the loss of a child at the hand of someone else was working with children who had been killed by a drunk driver. Rage is rage over the loss of a child.

Therapy was talk, talk, talk during the day and write, write, write during the night. The reliving of my life was like walking through a paper shredder. Dr. Doyle encouraged me to wear sunglasses when the therapy became too intense. I wore them without hesitation. It was difficult speaking the truth, and sometimes it was embarrassing, but it was necessary.

I had taken Wayne's advice and collected our used glass jars. When I would get a sack full, I would take them outside to the big trash can, throw them inside, and listen to them break. I would scream, yell, and curse. Why couldn't I wear sunglasses inside if it would help me walk over the hot coals of life and move forward in the grief process? The pain—physical, emotional, mental, and spiritual—was breaking me. I was the slave, and it was my master. I felt beaten and without hope. This had to change in order for me to want to go on with the rest of my life.

Carl went to a day of therapy with Dr. Doyle. He didn't want to discuss much about McKay, or our issues in the marriage, or his issues. He talked about issues that were not relevant to our healing. For example, the next day, Dr. Doyle relayed to me that Carl had told him I had run up the American Express bill to $10,000. I could not help but laugh as I told him, "I'm sitting here in old shorts, an old shirt, old tennis shoes, but a new Wal-Mart sweatshirt." I had asked Carl to drive me to Wal-Mart to get some sweatshirts because Tennessee was cooler than Texas. I told Dr. Doyle, "I could buy a lot of sweatshirts for $10,000!" I had not been shopping for clothes in a long time. The largest purchase I had made was for the suit I wore on the last day of the trial.

Carl had his issues, and I had mine. He related to Dr. Doyle the incident at the Woodlands Mall when I was overwhelmed and could not walk or talk. Dr. Doyle suggested Carl just walk off and leave me with my episode if it happened again. I later told Dr. Doyle that I had searched the Bible trying to find out how Jesus's mother got through the rest of her life after the crucifixion of her son. I grew angry at Dr. Doyle and told him that if Mary had had a spell at the New Jerusalem Mall, then maybe someone would have written about it and mothers who have lost their children would better know how to deal with the rage, anger, and brokenness. Finally, I had to make the decision to stop worrying and wondering how Mother Mary got through her life and to begin planning for how Paulette was to get through hers in a positive, proactive manner. I wasn't Mother Mary and Mother Mary wasn't me. I had to live own my life, just as Mary had lived hers.

Chapter Seven: 1996: Reality and Healing

There were three aspects I wanted to address during my therapy in Tennessee: my losses in childhood, my loss of McKay, and my anger at staying on earth instead of being allowed to stay in Heaven with McKay. Each one carried anger, but the combination of all three was staggering. The rocks in my sack were too heavy to carry. I was stumbling around and not making many positive tracks. It was time for me to change that course in my life, and only I could do that work to reverse the curse of all that had happened since I was born.

The greatest counsel given by Dr. Doyle was extremely sobering. He spoke this not only to me, but to Carl: "If you two don't do your work in therapy, then when life's circumstances bear down on you, or when a friend's child dies, and one will, Paulette, it will mean for you a return to the fetal position with speech and mobility problems, and Carl, it could mean for you severe health issues."

I didn't need to hear anything else. He commanded my full attention and commitment to the process of therapy. I did the work. I relived the pain and horror. I felt the feelings. I allowed myself to go to the depths of feeling that I thought McKay felt on the night he was taken. I allowed myself to feel the last moments of what I thought he felt when someone he loved delivered brutal cruelty and death. The feelings I felt were not McKay's actual feelings, but I did the best I could: I tried to visualize what I thought he must have felt and seen on that night. Once I returned to Texas, I again began meeting with Vernon, my local therapist. Most of my days and nights were spent alone. I did my painting and piano playing, I took care of McKay's blessed pets, and sometimes friends would stop by unexpectedly. That was a great respite for me. Some realtor friends would come for nearly free art lessons that occupied some of my time in the evening. Some friends would stop by and either bring food or jars to break or ask me to dinner. I seemed to be doing somewhat better after the intensive therapy with Dr. Doyle. I thought I was doing better at seizing the day, the moment, the second, and making the most of it while my feelings came and went. I tried to keep a positive focus on my mission in life. A friend reminded me recently that I was humbled when I was finally able to appreciate a cup of tea. The simple things began to bring some depth and stability back to my life.

Later, I returned to Dr. Doyle's for the second week-long intensive grief therapy session. I made a commitment that I was walking through therapy until I was told that I was at some point of completion.

To get away from the stress now and then during this period, I would travel to Mississippi. These trips were a comfort at times; at times they were unsettling. One trip comes to the forefront of my mind. It was to Wiggins, Mississippi, to the farm McKay loved. The town is old, and some of the streets are still paved from years ago. In the heart of the town is a gazebo park with a walking track, and there is a sign at the track that can be hung either way—but both sides say "Walk This Way." To keep down boredom while you walk, the town periodically changes the sign.

One evening during my visit, my sister and I were driving through town when we heard music. We followed the sound and came to the gazebo park. The music was from a sound system, and a group of people were having a church-type service under the gazebo. The group was a mixture of blacks and a few whites singing and listening to preaching. We stopped and listened for a moment. The children of the worshipers were playing in the dim light of the outer perimeter of the gazebo. The light was filtered by the trees, causing the figures to look like dancing silhouettes. The arms of the children were raised in the air—their legs dancing high to the beat of the music left me with the desire to return the next night.

That night we moved on to our destination. We were headed to a friend's to rock in an outside swing and enjoy the twinkling lights that were carefully laced through the trees. The moments I spent outside, swinging among the twinkling lights, were a grand time of escape from my world of horror and loss. I could swing and not focus on McKay and how he must have felt when he realized that his life was in jeopardy and near its end.

The next evening, I located a video camera and asked who wanted to go to the gazebo and watch and listen to the worship service. My sister and her stepdaughter and I drove back to Wiggins and had a most unusual evening. When we arrived, I moved out of the car and sat on a rail under the oaks. The preacher eventually noticed us. We had videoed some of the service when the preacher invited us to join them under the gazebo.

We did, and it gave me an opportunity to look into the eyes and faces of these beautiful people. The ladies wore tiny lace handkerchiefs atop their heads. They sang with a sincerity that moved me. We stayed for a while then moved on down the hill to the track. As we were walking, we heard someone yelling, "Sistas! Sistas!" We stopped, and a black lady dressed in Sunday best ran to us. She told us that she had a message from God for us.

First she spoke to my niece. She told her many things, and what she said caused her tears. She told my sister some of the circumstances of her life and that love conquers all. She looked deep into my eyes and said, "I know you think God has forsaken you, but He has a plan. He knows just where you are and what you need. He still loves you."

She asked if we would come back to the gazebo and pray with them. We said yes, and everyone gathered around. The preacher asked if anyone had a prayer request, so I told him I did. As I related quietly the circumstances of McKay's death, he prayed. Everyone prayed while we stood in the middle of the worshipers. When the praying stopped, the preacher said he had not known why God had pressed him to return to Wiggins, Mississippi, when earlier in his life he had vowed he would never return to Mississippi. He looked at the three of us and said, "Now, I know why!"

I've reflected on the words of the black lady. How did she know how I felt? We had never spoken before. I can still picture her running after us. Her dress fanned out and she looked as if she were floating down the hill instead of running. Her words were an ointment for me and my wounds. I felt that God had abandoned McKay, Carl, and me, until this gracious lady was willing to take a risk and speak her heart. I am most grateful for her gift.

The Foundation began a project, and I sat through the planning meetings and felt totally exhausted when they were over. I became more and more sure of my need for physical therapy and a good workout program. Dr. Doyle had suggested I work out three days a week. He told me to work out to a point of total exhaustion. The longer I went without a workout and physical therapy, the more I realized that he was right.

One evening after a planning session, I went with a friend to her workout. The gentleman who helped her with her physical therapy, Dave Holt, set me up for three nights a week. I hoped by working out before bedtime that I could possibly sleep. Sleep seemed to be the only relief from the intense stress I felt emotionally and physically.

The sessions were long and difficult because my body was rigid and sore. I usually stayed two hours, but I did not work out for the entire time. Some of the time was spent crying and resting because I was in a weakened state. My muscles and joints were tight and "stove up," as my grandmother would have said. I am most grateful to my trainer; when I thanked him for all his work and tolerance, he told me he was only a spoke in the wheel of my healing. Once he told me I was a survivor and that God would meet my needs. I was in one of my moods with God, and I was doubtful. I asked Dave, "if all you were receiving from the Master's table were crumbs, would you still feel the same?" But I continued the process of workouts, hot baths, massages, walking, reading, therapy, and praying.

The reading list from Dr. Doyle supplied me with ample suggestions. *Man's Search for Meaning, A Grief Observed*, and *Tracks of a Fellow Struggler* brought me out of my little box and helped me realize that suffering is a part of our human existence. I had become so wrapped up in my loss that I gave little thought to others who had suffered or were suffering at that point in time.

There was a shelf at the end of the bathtub where I placed the books I read. I purchased many of the books on the list, and other people generously purchased some for me. The stack grew over time as I read close to eighty

182

books on grief and loss. I understood from *Man's Search for Meaning* the desire to lay down and give up because of circumstances. From *A Grief Observed*, I related to holding onto hope and seeing all hope gone. *Tracks of a Fellow Struggler* revealed to me that even a pastor and his wife can lose a child. Each one brought to my world a story that ministered to me and helped prepare me for the long journey without McKay.

The combination of workouts, baths, and massages also brought some needed structure to my life. Church helped as well. Carl and I could not agree on church; I agreed with him that McKay had suffered and that God could have stopped Hilton, yet I knew that God gives humans choices. We wrestled with why there was not a flat tire, car trouble, or a change of heart, and we still wondered why there was no phone number on the night McKay was taken. I have reminded myself often that a series of decisions on that night were made by human beings. I was extremely angry at God, but I did not feel complete without worship. It was difficult to understand then, and I am not sure I understand it now. I think I had a depraved idea of God; I felt an inner need for Him, for the music of the old songs, for the scriptures being read and taught, and a time of surrender to an Almighty who towers above circumstances. I came to a peace with life and the uncontrollable circumstances that I faced daily, I accepted that I did not control anyone's destiny, and I did not control God.

The First Presbyterian Church in Conroe was a comfortable atmosphere for me. I had periodically attended there for several years. When McKay was young and Carl was out of town, we would visit this church. This is the church where McKay heard the Apostle's Creed, the Doxology, and the Lord's Prayer. When Carl would asked about church, McKay would respond, "Mom took me to the organized church!"

I wondered how I would feel going back to the Presbyterian Church. The first service I attended, I knew I was in the right place. The service began with "Surely the Presence," the same song I played for McKay, the same song that played as Carl and I touched McKay's casket and the Elvis blanket at the funeral home. I felt a peace that passed all understanding.

The services spoke to me weekly, and the congregation allowed me my space. Carl did not want to attend, yet he did not hinder my going. We usually met for lunch after the service. These were very lonely times for us, because in the past, church had been family time. I had often wondered how widows and women whose husbands would not attend church felt. I stepped into their world for a period of time each week. It was a lonely world, yet I knew I was not alone. It became a reflective time for me, and I began to feel as if Carl had died with McKay.

During this period of time, I became more aware of my surroundings. I didn't listen to TV for fear it would shock me backwards. I tried diligently to calm my life, to rest my body from unnecessary stress. Carl was different from me. He did not want to turn off the TV. He used it as a way to stay numb or as a lullaby to bring sleep. One day as I was dressing, I heard the family of the Unabomber making a televised apology. I listened intently, then *blip!*—Carl had chosen to turn off the TV. I asked him to turn it back on, and he asked why. I told him I would like to hear what a public apology from a criminal's family sounded like, because the Crawford family, to my knowledge, never issued a public apology.

The level of confusion grew as I listened to the sincerity of this man's family. They were apologizing for another family member's actions. I reminded myself that I should not forget the great contrast in the behavior of Hilton Crawford's family as opposed to the family of the Unabomber. I was later to learn that Hilton had returned home after leaving McKay's body in Louisiana. He spent time in his recliner, as he was not feeling well, while Connie spent time watching her recorded soap operas. At my home, there was wailing and chaos as people searched for the missing McKay. Neither Hilton nor Connie came to help or pay their condolences to Carl and me.

I traveled to New Orleans to visit Smokey and his family, and the realness of New Orleans touched me. Years ago, I had a moment frozen in time when a shadow cast among the partiers on Bourbon Street left me with a love of the city and those who visit. The shadow was from a statue of Christ, and it was cast across the crowd of those in costumes. This mirrored the love of Christ even for us in our sin. New Orleans is a place I love and long for several times a year.

Smokey's wife and I casually walked in and out of shops and galleries. One gallery was nestled down a small, open corridor. A piece of paper taped to an old window fluttered in the gentle breeze and caught my eye as we made our way to the entrance of the gallery. The paper read, "There is no way to judge the length of one's life!" I did not know who wrote the words or why or what prompted that person to tape it to the window. I only knew it held a deep message for me—the one who had once thought Carl, McKay, and I would all die in the proper order, and of course we would die peacefully in our sleep at a ripe old age. This slip of paper created a moment when I was teachable about the realities of life. I no longer think that people die peacefully; I no longer believe that we will all die of old age.

This tiny note caused me to begin to evaluate my thinking. I learned to stop myself and consider whether I was thinking straight or was in denial. I began to ask myself if I was making my days count for something. I might not conquer the world, but I could do something each day that was positive, loving, and done in sincerity.

I learned that God will allow us to be taught in the ways that will most likely touch us in a lasting way. If a person had voiced the information to me that day instead of leaving in on a slip of paper, I would probably have chosen to blow off their words or nod patronizingly. This tiny scrap of paper was like the Red Sea parting.

Smokey and his wife had a small wire angel hanging in their home. The angel was made by a local artist named Steve Martin and it was so beautiful that I wanted one for myself. Gail took me to the home of the artist. He lived in an old brothel in New Orleans, and it was being remodeled. The wooden steps were well worn. We entered his living quarters, and in the middle of the kitchen floor was a large pile of wire angels. I lost myself in the pile of wings and neoclassical faces. I floated in my moments with the angels. I smiled as I realized that I could not choose one angel over another. How does one do that? Making a decision during that time of my life was very difficult, and I could not choose. Months later, a package arrived from Smokey. Nestled inside the box was a mother angel and her baby made from wire.

Meandering in and out of art galleries in New Orleans is one of my favorite pastimes. The art covers a multitude of subjects and media. In one gallery, there were a series of paintings that I could relate to. The first one was of a bird's nest with a mom, dad, and child sitting inside the nesting area. A large bird was flying away with a piece of the nest in its mouth. From the painting one could surmise that the bird, by flying away, would dismantle the nest. The title of the painting was "Unraveled and Not Yet Revealed." I had wondered if any positive response could be made to McKay's death. This painting is a vivid image in my mind even to this day. I feel unraveled, and I still wonder what needs to be revealed about the death of a small child, the loss of relationship with a spouse, and the empty moments alone.

The pets were still affected by McKay's absence and my inability to walk them or overexert myself. I took care of their basic needs, but was not able to do much more than that. The winter was very difficult for me. My body was so stiff, and the cold water from the hose when I washed down the runs made me hurt even more. I reminded myself of Mother Teresa and her work of serving the poor. I would tell myself, *Do what comes next and shut up.*

Buffy, the oldest dog, a golden retriever, began a quick decline. She was overweight and did not move around easily. Several times I thought she would not make it through another cold day. She continued to survive even though her movements became slower and slower. One evening, I had taken her outside to stretch her legs, go potty, and get ready to bed down for the night. After she had walked a short distance, she lay down in the yard and would not move. My sister Patsy was trying to help me get her back inside.

My sister-in-law Tracey and her two sons stopped by to help. She also tried to help me lift her, but the three of us could not budge Buffy.

We called for extra help from a friend because the temperature was dropping, and we also felt she needed to go to the vet. My sister-in-law remarked that she had some donut holes in the car and that Buffy might move for a donut. We decided it was worth a try. One sniff and Buffy was up and going again. By the time Dave arrived, we had a good laugh amongst our tears as she ate the donut hole and lived another day. Within a few days, Buffy had to be put to sleep because her condition was hopeless—an inoperable bone spur on her spine had grown and pierced her throat. Carl sprinkled Buffy's ashes at McKay's gravesite. The loss for me was tremendous. It was another chapter closing in the book of my life. I felt as if things were out of control again and that death was running away with all that I loved and adored. I tried to remember all the memories we had as a family with Buffy, and I thought of the special moments when McKay and I would snuggle down with the pets and laugh and giggle and love our furry friends.

When Tigger the tabby cat died, I was so angry that I took the dead cat down to the cemetery to bury him there. An elderly lady stopped at the cemetery to check on me. When I finally told her what I was doing, she said, "I've never heard of that!" I hadn't heard of it either—I had never even thought of it, in fact, until I found myself in those circumstances. I realize now that each of us will do abnormal things during abnormal times. Each pet I've lost in my life has brought the words, "I won't give my heart away again!" but with time, I have learned to love again.

The five remaining pets left me with a sense of urgency to enjoy the time I had left with them. They were all getting old, and they were so treasured by McKay and me. They were a lot of work, but it is a great respect for each one of them that gave me the stamina to carry on and honor the role they had played in McKay's life and mine.

An invitation to appear on *Geraldo* came, and we accepted. I was not sure exactly how I felt about sharing personal feelings, but if our presence would heighten public awareness, then it would be worth the aches and pains and tears the appearance would cause. I have only seen a few seconds of the *Geraldo* program, and I only saw those because when I went for a medical test after the initial airing of the program, a TV was in the waiting room of the lab. When I was leaving, I glanced at the TV, and to my surprise, a rerun of the program was airing. I did not stop to watch. The pain was too much.

When we were in New York for the *Geraldo* program, we were treated very graciously. There was a penny on the floor in the room where we waited for our turn. The penny stirred courage inside me. There was a beautiful, young Jewish girl who helped me. Her name was from the Bible: Bathsheba. I could only smile and remark that if the Biblical lady was so beautiful, it was no wonder that King David stopped to stare. I see a parallel between King David's yearning for the beautiful Bathsheba, and Hilton Crawford's temptations with money.

While we were in New York, Carl, our attorney, his wife, and I visited the Metropolitan Museum of Art. Some of the paintings brought me to tears, especially one of Joan of Arc. Music and art stir my innermost feelings. We didn't really enjoy ourselves, as there was no way to squeeze fun out of a time when the loss was so fresh. I do not want to sound as if I didn't laugh during this time—I did. I enjoyed my moments at the museum, but my overpowering feelings of loss filled almost every part of my being. There were moments when even I rose above the loss and found humor in some of the circumstances. Our attorney, though competent, was not a fashion plate, and sometimes his choice of socks would catch my eye, and a chuckle would surface.

I continued playing golf, and now that I could play nine holes, my confidence took a giant leap. I had struggled for so long just to move about with some fluidity, and then I could play and walk part of nine holes of golf. I surprised myself since I had not played sports in high school.

My emotions were still rocky. The tears were like cloudbursts in a thunderstorm. A quietness, then a roll of rain that flooded the moment. Carl did not seem to know how to deal with me when he was at home. We ate out often. Both of us gained weight trying to relate over a plate of food. If we left to eat out or do anything, I would curl up into the fetal position as we drove home and entered our driveway. Carl's standard line was, "Don't do this to me, Baby!" I thought that was a strange response to the circumstances. I guess I expected him to be strong, and when he did not meet my expectations I just thought, "What a mess!"

During the winter months, I was especially vulnerable to falling apart. I could not get out and walk some days due to the weather, so I was more stressed than usual. One cold evening we went out to eat. I dressed warmly and wore one of my fluffy, fake furs. I don't own a real fur because I can't bring myself to wear a real animal. When we arrived home, I fell apart. Carl tried to help me from the car, and when he picked me up, I began to slip through the bottom of the fur. He is a large man who weighs almost 270 pounds, and the only way he could stop me from slipping through the coat was to push me against the car and put his knee between my legs. I can look back now and see the comedy in all of this, but at the time I was totally put out with God, myself, Carl, and of course everyone who was involved in the death of McKay.

The amount of time Carl spent at home grew less and less. He shifted the blame to many different areas instead of owning up to the fact that it was difficult to be in the home where McKay had lived. Many days when he was home, he would go to McKay's bedroom and lie in his bed for most of the weekend. I prayed and prayed that this cycle would stop because it was unhealthy for us both.

During this time, a friend's husband decided to leave her. He was confronted on his personal issues that had hindered family life and personal growth, and he chose to leave his wife and children instead of addressing his issues. The girlfriend I had depended on for support was now in need of my support, and I felt as if the blind were leading the blind.

She was crushed by her husband's decision. Many days she would not be able to function, and I would get in the car in my robe and rabbit-shaped house shoes, and the both of us would sit in her bed and drink diet cola, eat Goldfish crackers, and talk. We didn't solve any of the world's problems, and we certainly did not mend the broken marriage or bring McKay back, but we did talk. We learned a lot about each other that we did not know. I had no idea that she had been an avid reader of self-help books, as had I. When I asked her if she had done any reading about her husband's issues, she opened a cabinet and began throwing self-help book after self-help book my way. I had been blind to the person I called friend. We both had pridefully not shared the hurts in life—the real stuff that was ripping us and our families apart.

I began to realize that a friend is someone you can tell anything to. I began to tell her about what I had longed for all of my life, and of my new, different longings since McKay's death. I wanted to leave this earth and move on to a better place. I also shared with her the anger I felt toward Hilton and those who covered for him on the night McKay was taken. I would tell her what I would like to do to all of them. She was a sounding board for me, and when she said, "You can't do that!" I remained grounded in reality. She allowed me to speak my thoughts, which made me feel better. I didn't actually have to act on my emotions.

Being female and left alone, I was downright scared. Carl had returned to work, and most of his work was out of town. The house was so quiet. The solitude and quiet seemed to grow in volume as I would try to busy myself with tasks I could do. When my friend would call, I was usually in my robe and fuzzy rabbit-shaped house shoes. I was not more than a mile away, so I would go dressed in this attire. It was many months before I thought about what her neighbors must have thought when they caught a glimpse of the house shoes, but I really didn't care. My friend was hurting, and the reality of life is that some of us have even driven our children to school in our robes, uncombed hair, and rabbit house shoes.

Now, I can laugh—a little—at the humor in the circumstances that were so devastating at the time. I smile as I mentally recall the robe and the old house shoes. I weep as I recall the times I would jump on the bed trying to get my friend to get up and live again, not knowing how in the world I could encourage her when I was so empty myself.

Time passed. Circumstances changed and evolved, and we both returned to work and realized that life goes on. The first time I saw her smile was when she told me about a lunch she hat eaten at the local grocery store deli. She had gone there during her lunch break, and she saw a man having lunch by himself. When he completed his meal, he walked by her table and left her a rose he had sculpted from a white paper napkin.

I began teaching simple art lessons at night to my realtor friends. We kept it simple and enjoyed each other's company. I once again began to string beads, paint different types of boxes, and enjoy art as a way to bridge the gap between people. It was very healing for all concerned because the people who came had a great love for McKay. After McKay's death, Carl built me a trellis for the garden. It needed to be painted white, so I placed a can of white paint out with some cheap brushes, and when anyone would come to see me, we would spend some time painting the trellis.

I received a call from Carl one day. He informed me that the Louisiana coroner who worked McKay's case had died of a heart attack. This coroner was one of those who had created a great deal of frustration for me. According to those who were building the case against Hilton Crawford, this Louisiana coroner had apparently been less than professional in his responsibilities. I was disillusioned to find that anyone entrusted with his level of responsibility could and would act in a way that jeopardized the legal process and possibly prevented a criminal from receiving the maximum punishment by law. I can only say that I was not dismayed that he was gone. When he told me of the death, I replied, "Don't look at me. I've wanted to kill him myself, but I've been right here in my breakfast room stringing beads for my artwork."

Recently, the assistant of the deceased coroner contacted me. I described to her my frustration with the coroner, as he had told me at first that McKay had been shot in the head and it had not been a blunt trauma injury. The assistant explained the sequence of events and helped me understand why the coroner ruled the cause of death as he did. She assured me he'd been professional and thorough. I had wrestled with frustration toward the coroner for a long time, but the assistant put it to rest.

However, I still feel that there are six individuals who were sorely irresponsible in dealing with McKay from the night he was taken. I will be glad to know when they are gone.

I had a dream one night that I was in a beautiful park, and I came upon a glass wall. There was a bench, and McKay was sitting on it. He was wearing his trusty backpack, and in his hand, he held six crosses, the kind that are laid on top of a coffin at a Catholic funeral. He did not smile at me, but only held the crosses up and gently moved them back and forth. His eyes did not leave mine. His eyes said that I should not worry. He knew who the six people were. Then he spoke to me even though I did not hear him. His mouth said, "Go play!" and he continued to rock the crosses back and forth, back and forth. It was a moment that I carry with me daily.

Carl and I continued with therapy. I went regularly, and Carl went sporadically. I touched his forehead one day, and he ran from the house and left. He told me, "I cannot deal with these feelings!" One day Vernon, the therapist, asked if he could come visit my home. I showed him through the home and let him see McKay's areas. As we talked about McKay and his love for his home, I realized that Vernon had come with a mission in mind. He was obviously surprised that I would so readily show him McKay's areas of the house. Apparently, Carl had told Vernon that I did not go upstairs, and when I asked him if Carl had instigated his visit to our home, he said yes. I told Vernon that I regularly visited McKay's areas, and that I was making peace with the silence in my home. I realized then that Carl was shifting the attention from himself to me as a way to avoid his own feelings of loss.

I received a phone call from Wayne requesting that I allow him to introduce me to a family who lived in his neighborhood. I was open to meeting new people, but I certainly did not realize all that would be in store for me. The family had struggled with alcoholism and the recurrence of a family member's cancer. After meeting the couple, I would occasionally drive Jean, the cancer patient, to her therapist. The prognosis was not good, and it was determined that she would probably not live long. The time I did have with Jean was invaluable. I learned about living, dying, hospice, real friends, and severe physical pain.

In her last days, Jean sent for me. She was at home in bed and could do nothing but say her goodbyes and wait. When I went to visit with her that day, I thought of all our talks, and I remembered the time I filled her home with flowers because she had such a love for beauty. One sweet lady from church once did that for me, and it left a lasting impression, so in a tribute to her and the love she showed me, I passed on the beautiful deed to someone else. I thought of the silly fur hat from Neiman Marcus that Jean passed on to me. I have not worn it, but it now serves as a storage place for my new dog's toys. I remembered soberly the time I visited her without invitation and found her in agonizing pain. The pain was from the cancer treatments, and until that day, I had no idea the treatments would ever cause this much discomfort. She described the pain as knives slashing her flesh.

When I arrived for the requested visit during one of her last days, I was led to a bedroom where she lay, waiting. She was thin and looked old and tired. She was dying. Jean smiled and told me how much our friendship had meant to her, and she wished we had met early on in life. She gave a faint laugh and said something like, "If I make it through this time, we will go out to eat and have a party in about six months." When we said our goodbyes, I was nearly speechless; life had again thrown me a loss.

As I was leaving, the family shared with me some of the comments she had made during the last few days. Hospice had helped them understand that she had one foot here and one foot there. When I left their home, I realized that many times therapists work so hard to keep us focused on the here and now on earth. There were times immediately after McKay's death that I would talk of Heaven so much that it was evident that my heart was not on this earth. My daily longing had been for Heaven. When I visited with Wayne about the feelings I experienced during my last visit with Jean, I wept as I became more and more aware of the work that had been done to keep me moving in a positive direction and keeping both feet here on Earth. I spent many nights and early morning hours visiting with Wayne on the phone; he had a calming effect on me.

After some time had passed, I realized I was being left alone more and more often. Other than occasional visits from friends, and less frequent calls from my family, I was alone. I was particularly sensitive to dates . . . McKay's birthday, the anniversary of his death . . . these days were agonizing. On McKay's birthday, after his death, no one called but Wayne.

Although it was difficult, I accepted this as part of life and loss, and other people moving on with their lives. Having more time alone provided me space to reflect on my life with McKay and my life in general. The reality slowly sank in—I wasn't going to die as I once thought I would. I had actually welcomed the idea of death, and now I realized although I no longer feared it, I no longer wished for it.

The *Leeza Gibbons* show invited Carl and me to appear on national TV. The trip to California for me was a reminder of when McKay had said that when he was grown and gone, we could turn on the TV and see him where the words were on the rocks.

After Carl and I settled in the hotel, we opened the drapes and the word Hollywood that rests on the rocky hill was framed by the outer edges of the window. I said, "Why am I surprised?" McKay had told us that is where he could be found.

The trip was a quick turnaround, and I experienced a mixture of mental messages. I again wondered, *Is this time meaningful? Am I accomplishing something for children, or is it just entertainment for people who happened into a studio to see a talk show host or hostess?* I hope I have made a difference.

Chapter Seven: 1996: Reality and Healing

I have surrendered to the loss of a loved one. My acquiescence has not removed the anger, but it allows me to pull into the driveway without expecting a giggling little boy to greet me with, "What did you buy for me, Mom?"

Today, I go to visit a friend, the one who has not left my side emotionally since the beginning of this crisis. My body aches and I pray:

Help me to be loving and kind and remember that the deep anger can seep out and offend someone who is undeserving. Help me remember that McKay is in Heaven, no longer suffering. Help me surrender my life to serving my broken body, both physically and emotionally. Help me to be bold and honest. Let me give without expecting anything in return except the perseverance to continue moment by moment.

I have continued to write and collect, and my files grow thicker as I collect my thoughts and feelings. I now know that people whom I once thought trustworthy are not. The very few truly trustworthy ones have withstood the test of time. Moments of clarity not only sting my brain, they also sting my physical and emotional body. I try to erase in my mind what happened to McKay . . . anything but face the gut-wrenching truth. My only son has been ripped from this life, and no one on that night who could have intervened did.

One persistent thought I have is how to define the person of Hilton Crawford. He has been labeled names like predator, cold-blooded killer, and even a variety of gators and reptiles, but none of these seem to fill my need. I want to find a word that I feel adequately describes him. One day, I happened upon the word *bomb.* Webster defines the word as "a hollow case filled with something that can explode." This fits. There was certainly an explosion in all our lives—McKay's, Carl's, and mine—by a hollow case filled with what? Rage? Anger? Jealousy? Greed? Or maybe . . . no emotion at all?

I don't understand why this mental and rather emotional exercise seems so important, and understanding the dynamics of our catastrophic loss is beyond me. I have accepted the fact that healing is a long-term process I will never fully understand. My job is to adapt to my new emotional surroundings and ascend to a level of acceptance that McKay is gone, and I am forever changed. The so-called ascension to acceptance is painful, especially during the nights when I awaken after having dreamed about McKay. The pain is unbearable as I sit in McKay's great-grandmother's rocking chair and cry for hours.

Therapy was still a required part of the process of healing, and there was no choice other than to walk through the pain. Both were healing—therapy and pain walking. I learned a new vocabulary as I traveled the road to healing. One example was the word *flex*, which means I should not try to control, but instead allow God to unfold my days. This became my motto until more buried anger would surface, and then I would say that flex meant adjusting to all my shattered hopes and dreams. When that kind of rage resurfaced, I would experience the debilitation of my previous stroke; my left side would pull and ache, my right foot would drag, and my speech would get sluggish. Although these physical signs gradually reduced from the full force I had experienced in 1995, they did continue to recur from time to time.

The massage therapists I used had noticed an improvement in the stiffness and rigidity of my body as I relaxed during the massages. I recall one session that was especially difficult as I waited for the therapist in the room feeling so alone and abandoned by God. Suddenly, I was aware of a faint figure that appeared at the end of the table. I strained my eyes and looked directly into the face of a man whose being was a misty gray-white. At that moment, a calm surrounded me and an inner peace replaced the feelings I had experienced only moments earlier. The figure drifted and moved to a wall until no longer visible.

The first masseuse I had in 1996 told me not to be surprised if I had a spiritual revelation in the future. When I questioned her, she said she had known many people who grew spiritually during their treatments. Since then, I have kept this moment in time in my mind, reminding myself of the misty face associated with the vision. The memory floods my soul with that same calm peace I felt at the time I saw him.

I wanted to have a life in which I would not be so dependent upon Carl or anyone else for my well-being. It was time to take ownership of me—the good and the not so good. I felt like I were beginning again, and again, and again, due to circumstances in my life but beyond my control. I became more and more restless to move forward, but my body was not cooperative.

One troubling period came when I found myself dwelling on the fear of McKay's ashes coming home. I thought that if McKay's ashes were stored here, in the house, I might be tempted to wrap them in a baby blanket and rock them in my kitchen rocker. I asked Carl, for my own well-being, to place the ashes in the bank lockbox.

One evening just after dark, I was finishing up in my office. I heard the back kitchen door open, and seconds later I heard Carl's scream. I immediately ran to him, thinking someone had again invaded our lives and space in order to harm us.

When I reached the kitchen, Carl was holding a tiny box wrapped in white paper. A neighbor who meant well had received a call from the funeral home, picked up the ashes, and delivered them to our door without advance warning. I was both angry and sorrowful that Carl and I were denied the moment of picking up and holding the ashes as a couple and as McKay's mom and dad.

This reminded me that, due to outside interference, Carl and I had not grieved McKay's loss together. Sometimes people thought they were making the best decision for us when, in fact, Carl and I were quite capable of thinking and reasoning for ourselves. The therapist would say that we were probably the most "aware" couple in the state.

Contrary to my earlier fear, I did not wrap the ashes in a blanket, nor did I rock them. They were the ashes of our precious child, but they held no spirit, no spirit at all. I could not even relate with these ashes, and they were taken to the lockbox.

Later, I decided to work for Wayne and travel to Mexico, which meant retrieving my passport from the bank lockbox where the ashes were stored. It was a hurdle to be faced. I went to the bank—my heart raced. I wanted to turn around and run out, but I knew I had to obtain the passport. The room was quiet—so quiet it was overwhelming. In this time of decision, I slowly turned the key in the lock. There it was—the little box holding my son's ashes. I carefully reached around it to secure the needed passport, closed the door, and relocked the box. Instead of the dreaded moment of cowardice, it became a moment of a new courage.

I have requested that at my death I be cremated, my ashes mingled with those of McKay's. I would like us to be divided and scattered in three places— White Oak Creek; Wiggins, Mississippi (the place McKay referred to as the most beautiful place on earth); and at the gravesite.

The second Family Field Day held by the McKay Foundation in the spring of 1997 was successful, yet I knew we were only reaching a small portion of the population. The message of McKay's abduction and murder needed to be spread quickly to as many homes as possible because the reality was, if this could happen to McKay, it can and may happen to anyone.

The question was how to spread the word. I had spoken to a college psychology class, and one mother in the class commented that she did not want to frighten her children with information concerning safety. It was obvious that the mom was focusing on her fears. I told her, "Your fears can kill your children."

When do we allow our fears to hinder us from making good decisions for our families and ourselves? I have learned that if I feel feelings of fear, I need to step back and evaluate the situation. Sometimes we need to make decisions that will make someone else unhappy. We are taught to be people pleasers and that means no one should be unhappy because of our decisions, but this urge to be nice is not realistic . . . it's dangerous.

For a time, everything seemed to symbolize grief. The pouring rain seemed like the downpour of tears I had shed. I shared a concern with Carl during this time: I thought that any future life circumstance would be compared with the loss of McKay, and the new issue would dim in significance.

I now realize that God does not always change the course of events. He only walks through them with us. He was the only one constantly with me as I walked through the valley of the shadow of death, through the days of desolation as I lived alone in a big house once home for a precious little boy.

The days were like a journey to hell. The emotional and physical ramifications commanded my attention, and I had no doubt that Hilton Crawford or anyone else connected with the abduction and murder of McKay deserved death in return.

Each day was a new chapter. I made a decision to travel by car to the Carolinas with Wayne—a beautiful ride. I had never visited the area before and understood why Billy Graham called it "God's Country." Along a back road, we passed a quaint and whimsical garden with furniture made from bent willow. I learned it was called Victoria's Garden. We saw a garden made from wrapped and twisted branches. I'm not sure what caught my eye first, but a flowing stream ran through the garden, the music of the garden was that of birds and the running stream, light filtered through the trees and cast shadows that only intensified the mystique and beauty of someone's busy but creative mind, and a rabbit hopped through. Not a typical looking rabbit, but one that looked like a long-haired white dog with rabbit ears. A thistle was caught in its fur. He was busy with twigs too.

A turtledove was perched on a ledge of a window box. It was an unusual site, for behind the window box was a window that overlooked a room decorated with a mural of the forest and stream. It gave the garden much charm and created somewhat of an optical illusion.

The garden's namesake was a beautiful child named Victoria, the granddaughter and younger version of her grandmother, the creator of the garden. The grandmother allowed us a closer look at the garden, as some areas were not visible from the road. A swing had been fashioned from branches, and it was impossible to visit and not swing. To this day, when I want to relax, I think of the beautiful garden, the charming namesake, and a grandmother who expressed her love by creating beauty and tranquility and naming it for a child.

From time to time, the pressure was increased on others involved in McKay's death and new information would surface. One afternoon at dusk, I was home alone. Carl was working out of town, and he had called me. As we chatted on the cordless phone, a college-age Caucasian male walked up the back driveway and rang the doorbell. When I answered the door, he was holding a small spray bottle in one hand and a cloth in the other. He told me he was selling spot remover. The young man at the door asked if he could come in and demonstrate his product, so I told Carl to hold on a few minutes while I talked with the person at the door.

I told the man I could not allow him in my home. I was holding the phone out from my ear so Carl could hear some of the conversation. The salesperson said he would come in and clean the worst spot I had on my carpet, and when I told him no, he smiled a cocky smile and said, "I don't know why you won't let me come in and clean your carpet. I just cleaned Mrs. Crawford's floor. You know Mrs. Crawford, don't you?" I told him I did not know a Mrs. Crawford, and he turned and left.

Carl came home that night. We didn't know how to respond to this event, so I notified the district attorney's office of this and other similar events so that the information might be placed in a file. To my knowledge, there has been no investigation of this incident.

In June of 1997, I was invited to speak for the Foundation in Washington DC, before the Caucus on Missing and Exploited Children. A Foundation board member and I traveled together. The two of us are as different as night and day, but we both welcomed the privilege of visiting many US congressmen concerning prevention education for children. We visited the Center for

Missing and Exploited Children, and our moments in Washington were lonely and puzzling. I pondered over whether my speaking would bring about any change or a new enlightenment.

My faith was not high when I considered man's system of caring for children and holding others accountable for their actions toward children. Too much talk and not enough action seemed to be the mode where children were concerned. I was amazed to learn that the laws at the state level were very lax concerning pedophiles. Many pedophiles do not seem to respond to rehabilitation, yet are freed to roam the streets after a slap on the hand. The cost to society for criminals to roam the streets and prey on children is high— some research says 16 times more costly than prevention. I have become more and more convinced that a special prison should be constructed that would house only pedophiles. It would be a safer environment for children if these predators were imprisoned and not allowed to be near children ever again. I extend no mercy to those who would harm a child in any manner. I realize now that our system has its flaws, and that the community at large has allowed the voice of a few not to be heard. The few—those who feel that child molesters, pedophiles, abductors, and murderers of children have been a pathogen to society far too long and should be put away forever—aren't heard.

Every instinct I had in me had been to protect my son. I knew the world was full of predators who can cripple and destroy the lives of children, and I was a realist, but I was not real enough to realize that this horrible thing could happen to McKay by someone he loved.

I requested information on all known pedophiles in Montgomery County, and one day, long after I had forgotten my request, a very large packet came by mail. I looked at the return address and wondered what the sheriff would be sending me. It was the information I had requested, and I was sickened as I read the names and the nature of the crime. I was even more sickened to learn that they are not in jail. They are free. This evil person may be the one who mows your lawn, the person who cleans your pool, the person who changes the oil in your car, the person who teaches your child, or the person who preaches to you on Sunday. I do not live in fear, but I do live in deep awareness of the level of evil my son faced on the night he was taken.

Life seemed to be a large jigsaw puzzle with lots of pieces to put in place. Every day, I wondered, "Why, God?" The ageless wisdom in the Bible seemed so alive, and yet there wasn't any one part I could hold on to. I remember the times of watching TBN on television. Religion has confounded me for years, and I would pause and listen from time to time. I would hear snippets that came to mind after McKay's death, and I realized that life's events can give vision. For example, Dottie Rambo, a religious songwriter, shared her experiences about her health problems. She said she had prayed Jesus would walk close enough to her to drag the hem of His garment over her because she was too weak to reach up and touch it. It would never have occurred to me to pray in this manner, but after McKay's death, I knew that level of weakness and need.

In one instant of time, I went from memorizing scripture to forgetting everything I had memorized and not knowing how to pray. There was a great battle inside my head. My heart still leaned on God, but my knowledge was dimmed, and my heart was broken.

I would remind myself that God is in control of this earth even when everything seemed to be out of control. It reminded me of a series of unexplainable events that began in my senior year of high school. A friend of mine had a glossy, black-and-white picture of the person who played Jesus in *Jesus Christ Superstar*. Although I was not a fan of this musical, I looked at the photo and said, "I'll meet him one day."

During the trial, I found out that the same man was speaking at a church in Huntsville, and I asked Carl to drive me back to Huntsville to hear him speak. The gentleman no longer sang rock, but he spoke and sang in churches. Carl was not open to the idea of my going to see this man.

Then, on a return flight from Memphis where I went to my first intensive grief therapy week, Carl and I were waiting in the terminal. Much to our surprise, in walked this man: Jeff Fennholt. After takeoff and when the plane reached its maximum altitude, I told Carl I had to have a delayed visit with Jeff. We visited, and I shared with him the events of my life and the full circle of knowing we would one day meet. He in turn shared with me some of his life's struggles. Even though our meeting was not explainable in human terms, I looked at it from a world that is God-controlled and knew that even when events seem out of control, anything is possible through God's plan.

One day during the winter, I walked to the carriage house where Carl was working at the back of our property. I had decided I was ready to work again with him in his office upstairs in the carriage house. At this time, I still dealt with severe physical fatigue, and it was standard for the afternoons to be a time of very slow movement for me; I was also getting bored. I decided to approach Carl with my decision to return to work.

I found him working, and he stopped long enough to listen to my request. I told him I was ready to work again although I could not do much. I offered to do simple tasks like addressing envelopes, but he informed me that I wasn't welcome in the company. This was the company I held ownership in! At this moment, I felt terribly abandoned and alone. The walk back to the house was long as the reality of my new life with Carl was beginning to soak in. I had no son, no job, and no husband.

Wayne had become my safety net, and I worried that there were times he was there because of pity. I called him and told him what had happened when I tried to talk to Carl about returning to work. He said, "Let it go, you have a job." I was puzzled by his comment, and I asked him, "What job?" He laughed and told me I could design gift items for his company. I asked him to explain what he was talking about, and he said the gift items would be produced in Mexico then marketed through the gift market in the United States. I asked him how much he could pay me, and although it was not much, it was a job.

I also found work at a gift shop unpacking boxes of merchandise. I could do this for only short periods of time. The business, called Oogie's, was owned by a really neat family. I worked when I could and used it as a time to get out of the house. The ladies who owned the shop agreed to show and sell my art in return for my time. They were most gracious and are a treasured memory in my healing. Sometimes I would work an hour in the morning, sometimes longer. Regardless, it was work, and to me, work was a healthy release.

I was ready to do more than unpack boxes, and I was emotionally crushed by Carl's insensitivity. I was broken, and I did not have the energy to stand up to him. I did not realize that a display of anger and frustration in taking a stand in rejoining a company I had helped establish would have given me a moment of nurturing a seed of strength. In hindsight, I am glad he told me what he did. It saved me much trouble.

I began working with Wayne. We drove to Monterrey, Mexico, to visit the factory and design the prototype gift items. The trip was eventful. The diligent workers in the factory were eager to please, and together we designed items and made plans for publishing a catalog in Mexico.

While in Monterrey, we visited a brass factory, and walking in the door, we felt like we were stepping back in time to the turn of the century. At this outdated, unsafe factory, we were either walking on dirt floors or walking on ill-constructed catwalks made from planks and cinder blocks. Large vats about twice the size of a chest-type, deep freezer were filled with brass and heated with a fire made from wood. The heat and fumes caused my eyes to sting. The items that were made were of good quality and design, but it was difficult to imagine spending a lifetime of teenage and adult years in these types of working conditions. I asked Wayne why he took me to a factory run in such dire poverty, and he mumbled something about increasing my level of thankfulness. We did not use the labor or materials from this sweatshop-type factory.

The items that were manufactured in Mexico were marketed and sold in the gift markets in Chicago, Atlanta, Dallas, Los Angeles, New York, Boston, Kansas City, Seattle, and Pittsburgh. The trips I made to each of these cities was an adventure. I had fun, but it was also a time of physical and mental exhaustion. I did not feel I was much help to Wayne, but he was in good humor and very willing to help me carry my load.

Even though deep depression was a daily part of my life, I tried to remind myself to enjoy the moment and to find something to laugh about and something fun to do each day. At one of the markets, I rolled a golf ball to Wayne to let him know I had arrived. He is an avid golfer and to see a little white ball rolling down the aisle brought a big smile to his face.

When I arrived at the Atlanta market, I heard piano music. A black baby grand was in my path, and as I entered the piano space, the pianist began to play "Memory" from CATS. Again, the song McKay and I loved ministered to me. I was overwhelmed with emotion, and I sat on the piano bench with the pianist. As he played, I told him of McKay and of the significance of the song he was playing. I was blessed by the timing of this song. As he finished, he told me he would not forget the moments we shared, nor would he forget McKay; the song would have new meaning for him.

The size of the marketplace caught me off guard. Wayne had given me detailed instructions on how to locate him, but my listening skills were and are in much need of improvement. I dressed trying to look professional, not knowing that I would lose my way for half a day. I hadn't thought about the strain high heels and luggage would place on my body. By the time I found Wayne, I had beat up my legs with the luggage and still had bruises the next day. Wayne and I went to a restaurant, dragging my luggage and some gift items he needed to keep with him. The restaurant was crowded, and we were to be seated at the far back corner. The hostess suggested we enter from a different door, so we followed her and did not think about an alarm sounding when the door to the alternate entrance was opened. Even though I was wearing high heels and carrying a tote bag, I rushed across the restaurant because alarms, sirens, or loud noises caused me to have a severe panic attack.

When it registered in my brain that I was not in danger and that I was running to nowhere and away from Wayne, I came to an abrupt stop. I looked down into the face of a man who was eating alone. He had lesions on his neck and face.

The moments slowed and so did my pulse and impulse to run as we looked deeply into each other's eyes. The man smiled at me, and I smiled back. Everything stopped, but there was an unspoken understanding—this moment in time brought an clarity to my thoughts I can't put into words.

We completed lunch, and as we were walking back to the market, Wayne asked me to swap my tote for something lighter: a glass tray. His instructions were, "Don't drop it!" It was shortly thereafter that the package hit the sidewalk with a boom. Wayne looked at me, and I responded with something like, "Don't say a word." I picked up the package and moved on. In my head I said, "Philadelphia!"

The word Philadelphia had gained significance while I was in Monterrey, Mexico, having lunch with the owner of the factory, his wife, and their priest. In an effort to be cordial to everyone, I tried to visit with each person at the lunch table. I speak no Spanish, and I was trying my best to get along in a country where I did not speak the language. I asked the priest if he spoke English, and he smiled, raised his hands, and said loudly, "Philadelphia!" I thought, this is just great—I speak no Spanish, and all he can say is Philadelphia. What a great conversation this will be. It was funny, yet frustrating.

The priest went on to say something in Spanish to the others, and they translated for me that he had once visited in America in the city of Philadelphia. Since then, when I get frustrated with a new task you might hear me say "Philadelphia," and laugh!

The work, the time, the experience, and all of the money that Wayne expended—all of it ended in a colossal flop. I cannot express enough gratitude to Wayne for what it did buy for me: a beginning of regaining my confidence and of trying something new. It was a fun learning experience that would hold some wonderful memories that I could return to when the stark realities of McKay's death pressed down on me.

My time in Monterrey and working in the gift industry caused me to reflect on a time in 1996, when, with Carl's help, I tried to locate a gallery in which to hold an art show. I was trying to decide how to use my talents to bring home income and yet maintain a somewhat stress-free environment because of my health.

Although the galleries were booked, I made a decision to have the show in December as a way to get through the holidays. A gentleman who owned a frame shop in Houston most graciously offered his beautiful facility for the show. I painted, strung beads, and created art that helped in my healing. One piece disturbed Carl. In it, I used a technique I learned from a New Orleans artist. In the piece, Carl was in the likeness of Elvis, McKay was a toddler, and I was represented in the background as a skeletal face. In a frightened voice he asked, "Paulette, what does this mean?" His question caused me to pause and consider many things about myself, especially self-doubt. I realized the art I was creating was changing me, and that change was making some people uncomfortable with me. I was more willing to express myself, even in my art.

The art show was a defining moment when I realized I was a "starving artist." Though I had some natural talent, it was not—nor would it be—profitable, nor would it be a form of making ends meet financially. I knew then that I needed to find a good job. Hindered by a lingering fatigue, how would I rebuild my life, physically, emotionally, mentally, and spiritually?

The time came when I realized I couldn't keep everything Carl and I had been given when McKay was taken. I didn't relish the idea of looking at all the cards, booklets, and letters that were boxed and stored out of sight. There were between two and three thousand pieces of mail to sort through. Before I could part with the gifts and McKay's possessions, there was much to be touched, smelled, and wept over. I began the process by bringing the boxes and cards downstairs. I called my girlfriend, Bitsy, seeking her help for the long evening ahead. The FBI had informed us that it was best to destroy as much as I could stand to destroy. We were warned about those who might pass the letters and cards on or sell them to peddlers and profiteers. This was during the time of the sport-type cards on criminals. In order to spare ourselves this type of hurt, I made the decision to reread the cards and letters before burning them. I had decided that Carl would avoid this decision for a lifetime if he could, so it would be up to me to muster the courage to try to do something. I went to the barn and found a container suitable for burning—a mailbox.

The weather was good for what we were doing, so we read until the upturned mailbox was nearly full. As we read, we stopped and talked about what people wrote, and we even found a check that had been overlooked. Some of the cards were uplifting, some comments were touching, and in some, to be honest, we couldn't quite understand what was written. Nevertheless, we recognized their sincerity. Many cards and letters were from other mothers who had lost children. They were written with a level of understanding that brought a kinship in our lives.

As the time ticked by, Bit and I were sometimes silent and sometimes talkative, but we both changed after that evening on the back porch. We watched the tiny embers of memory rise in the air as we placed each card in the mailbox incinerator.

In late winter of 1997, after having begun to weed out McKay's personal things, there came a night when I no longer selectively gave away his things. It was a night to remember. I became more and more human as I came across his little personal treasures. I had wondered what it would be like to clean out, and when I would be able to do so. These two words—clean out—seem disrespectful to McKay, yet that is exactly what was happening. I cleaned out. I have wondered since, as I did on that night, why we as humans have not established better names for sacred rituals. We have failed humanity in this area.

I chose one particular night when I was sick with a flu-like bug to begin the sorting process. I convinced myself that it would be better to do this when I was feeling really terrible than beat myself up on an evening when I was feeling better. I asked myself, *What do I do with all the "stuff" this little person accumulated?* The reality was that a lot of the "stuff" had to be touched, smelled, and parted with . . . all part of the grief process.

I had gotten McKay's closet cleaned out when I received a couple of calls from friends. The weather was rainy, and the cold and drizzle did not add anything positive to the evening since it was a reminder of the rainy evening McKay was taken. Wayne called to find out if I was okay because he knew rainy weather sent me into a deeper depression as I repeatedly wondered, *Is this the sound McKay heard on that night?*. I told Wayne what I was doing, and why I was doing it that night. Wayne asked if I would like some help, and he offered his services, along with his son Trent's. I accepted their help, and when they arrived, they asked me what I planned to do with McKay's things. I told them I was driving them to the Salvation Army the next morning. Wayne told me I had done enough, so he and Trent loaded the things I had cleaned out.

They then asked what else I would like to clean out, and I mentioned McKay's bathroom. They quickly completed that task and loaded everything into the car. Wayne's yacht of an old car still had room left, so he and Trent asked if I wanted to continue the cleaning out process. I did, and we went up to the attic. This room was as difficult to clean out as any of the other areas. It was a walk-in attic, and McKay's Christmas tree stood there, proudly decorated. To see it there, I felt as though it were being stuffed down my throat. I felt as if I would fall on my face, and I lost my breath for a split second when I saw it. It had brought McKay so much pleasure.

I had given quite a few of the stuffed animals away to the church library and to the college library, but there were still more to clean out. We loaded Wayne's car until there was no more room. I felt drained as Wayne and Trent drove off. They agreed to deliver the items to the Salvation Army the next morning.

I went back to the attic and realized that there were still things to be cleaned out. The Christmas tree for one, but that was more than I could take. I called my brother Paul and asked him if he would take the tree for his son, Halen. I told him if he wanted it, he would have to come right then and there, no questions asked. He came immediately and took the tree, the snoring Santa that my mother had given McKay, and McKay's costume collection.

So, one evening of the flu bug, and almost all of McKay's things were gone. There was little remaining except in the hidey-hole/computer/play room, which stored my most favorite possessions that belonged to McKay. His violin and some of his sheet music were sent to a local artist who owned a frame shop to create a collage in tribute to McKay's musical ability. The piece that was created is amazing and hangs in my music room today. I had his golf glove framed, the same one he had used during his life and I had used after his death. The glove is well-worn, but most precious to me. The poem "If," by Rudyard Kipling, hangs behind the glove. The poem's line "If you can keep your head when all about you/are losing theirs and blaming it on you" has always meant a lot to me. The playbill from the New York trip to see *The Messiah* is framed and hanging.

These are my most prized possessions and I did not want to misplace them or store them away. I want them in my sight where I can feel again the moments with McKay. I did not want to put out a few photos and forget the positive times. I wanted to acknowledge his wonderful presence in my life and live healthily with my loss. He was so very important to me. Why would I hide my greatest prize in some box in the attic or under a bed when this was a beautiful life that needed to be celebrated? I did save a few other items of McKay's, but I did not want to have them framed. I had to draw a line somewhere and set some boundaries because I did not want my home to become a shrine.

"Cleaning out" is difficult. Whenever I clean out a closet, the pantry, or the refrigerator, I am reminded of the cleaning out that I had to do in order to move on. I had to take one more step that night in my growth. I had to accept that McKay would not be wearing the clothes, but some child at the Salvation Army might need what was just hanging around. McKay would not be playing with the toys, but some child would smile to get one of them. There were other children who had needs, and McKay's possessions could help some other child. He would have approved of my decision.

Moving on was extremely difficult, but what else could I do? I had to grow up.

That weekend, when Carl came home, I did not tell him about cleaning out McKay's things for the first few hours. I wanted him to be home without knowing. When I did tell him, he cried and ran for his suitcases. I called him and asked him if he was mad at me, and he said he wasn't, but that he couldn't deal with the feelings he was having.

My heart was being tugged as my third Christmas without McKay approached. I thought about the times McKay and I had discussed the Salvation Army and its mission. It was only fitting that his possessions be given to the Salvation Army. McKay and I had plans to ring the bell for the Salvation Army at Christmas. McKay didn't make it, but I decided I would give some time to ring the bell in front of the local Wal-Mart store. It was a shocker for some of the people I knew. They would drive by and lower their car windows and ask what I was doing. I would ask them what it looked like I was doing and tell them that I needed some money for the Salvation Army. Some treated me as if I had flopped over the edge of social etiquette. One person on the McKay Foundation's board said if I thought I was going to get anything accomplished for the Foundation by ringing that bell, I was mistaken. I was shocked at her response. I wasn't ringing the bell for the Foundation, I was ringing it because it was what I had planned for the holidays with McKay. Ringing the bell helped me find a time of closure and healing. It was a time to move on and learn. It was a time to become more and more aware that I had to chart my own course in life. It was a time of realizing that some people would not like my choices and would make ugly comments.

I am thankful for the relationship I had with McKay. It blessed my life and influenced me to become who I am today. I learned from McKay to be me, to live the moment, and to appreciate every breath. I will continue to struggle in my life. Great moments in time come to all of us when, in a backward glimpse, we find the courage to look forward toward the unknown future—a future known only by God.

I don't want to be a big fish in a little bowl. I want to swim in the oceans. I want to do more to make sure boys and girls are safe.
—Paulette, 2005

Epilogue

September 12, 2005,
Tenth Anniversary of McKay's Abduction and Murder

Today marks ten years since McKay's abduction and murder. I am on a plane going to a convention where I will present the safety curriculum developed by The McKay Foundation. This is the first trip on which I will go alone. I feel stronger now, but I have questioned whether or not I am ready to face speaking and the anniversary date at the same time. I remind myself that I have walked on the hot coals of losing McKay, walked through a divorce, suffered a stroke, endured the trial and witnessed the execution, viewed not only the files of the criminal case but also the photos of McKay's remains, and lived the moment-by-moment existence that comes with facing tragic loss. I convince myself that I am ready to move on to the next chapter in my life.

Today you may be facing a great loss in the form of death, divorce, disease, or a multitude of other heart-wrenching life experiences that can leave you forever changed.

It is my prayer for you—wherever you are in your journey—that you may hold fast and take courage.

Sincerely,

Paulette

The McKay Foundation
www.protectingchildren.org